THE CLASH *In Their Own Words*

Nick Johnstone

The Clash "Talking"

OMNIBUS PRESS

THE CLASH *Talking*

ISBN13: 978.1.84609.400.2
ISBN: 1.84609.400.3
Order No: OP51425

Exclusive Distributors:
Music Sales Limited,
8/9 Frith Street, London W1D 3JB, UK.

Music Sales Corporation,
257 Park Avenue South, New York, NY 10010, USA.

Macmillan Distribution Services,
53 Park West Drive, Derrimut, Vic 3030, Australia.

To the Music Trade only:
Music Sales Limited,
8/9 Frith Street, London W1D 3JB, UK.

Photo credits:
Front cover: Sipa Press/Rex Features; back cover: LFI.

All images courtesy of LFI except:
Andre Csillag/Rex Features: 42, 49, 54, 100, 128; Ian Dickson/Redferns: 71; EVT/Rex Features: 38;
PRE/Rex Features: 50, 64, 106, 109; Brian Rasic/Rex Features: 81, 84; Ebet Roberts/Redferns: 30, 92, 97, 112;
Lex Van Rossen/Redferns: 105; Sipa Press/Rex Features: 59, 108; Ray Stevenson/Rex Features: 23, 27, 75, 76, 79;
STI/Rex Features: 43; Richard Young/Rex Features: 22.

Colour Section: Andre Csillag/Rex Features: 2; Nils Jorgensen/Rex Features: 3; LFI: 4, 5, 6, 7, 8; Rex Features: 1.

Every effort has been made to trace the copyright holders of the
photographs in this book but one or two were unreachable.
We would be grateful if the photographers concerned would contact us.

Printed by: Caligraving Limited, Thetford, Norfolk.

A catalogue record for this book is available from the British Library.

Visit Omnibus Press on the web at www.omnibuspress.com

CONTENTS

❝We came, we made music, we exploded.**❞** JOE STRUMMER, 2002

❝The striking thing about The Clash was that, as universal as their appeal grew to be, all the influences in their music could be attributed to a few square miles of London. When I think of them, I think of Ladbroke Grove in West London. I can see the doorways and the record shops. I can remember the smell of the Jamaican restaurants.❞ BONO, 2004

Over five classic albums, one resounding dud of a sixth (as The Clash 'Mk. II') and a slew of ground-breaking singles and EPs, The Clash burned brightly and briefly, before imploding in a mire of drug problems, ego tussles and inter-band politics. During their short lifetime, they blazed a pioneering trail, breaking early from the confines of the British punk scene to embrace first black music (chiefly reggae), then American music at large (rockabilly, rhythm 'n' blues, rap, jazz, Motown), before synthesising their influences and marrying them to a raggedy white guitar driven rock 'n' roll template.

Introduction

By the time that journey was complete, drummer Topper Headon was wrestling heroin addiction, Joe Strummer and Mick Jones were butting heads over who was the real 'star' of The Clash, Paul Simonon was going with the flow and the band's latest and biggest selling album to date, *Combat Rock*, was riding high in charts worldwide. They had come a long way from the squats and club gigs of 1976. Perhaps too far. A year later, in 1983, Strummer and Simonon kicked Mick Jones out of the band, effectively killing off The Clash. Initially, Strummer, Simonon and three faceless musicians soldiered on as The Clash Mk. II, releasing the universally panned *Cut The Crap* album, before wisely calling it a day in 1986.

The Clash came together in 1976, when Bernie Rhodes, then semi-managing a Paddington band called London SS, dragged co-founding member Mick Jones (born London, June 26, 1955), fledgling bassist Paul Simonon (born Thornton Heath, December 15, 1956) and lead guitarist Keith Levene (later of Public Image Ltd) to see The 101ers, a London pub rock band. On seeing the wired stage presence and boundless charisma of 101ers frontman Joe Strummer (born John Graham Mellor, Ankara, Turkey, August 21, 1952), the London SS crew invited Strummer to jump ship and join their band. Strummer, who had recently seen The Sex Pistols and realised that punk was what made his heart beat faster, didn't even have to think about it. A few rehearsals and band names later, Simonon crowned them The Clash. With Terry Chimes (born London, January 25, 1955) on drums, they made their live debut in Sheffield on July 4, 1976, opening for The Sex Pistols (a logical move since Bernie Rhodes had long known the Pistols' manager Malcolm McLaren).

Over the next year, Levene left the band, punk broke into the mainstream, The Clash took off on The Sex Pistols' Anarchy tour at the end of 1976, entered the following year signed to CBS records for a £100,000 advance and unveiled their anthemic debut single, 'White Riot' in March 1977. They also perfected an iconic image for themselves – a mix of clothing from Portobello market sprayed with slogans and turned their live show into one of the hottest around. When their debut album *The Clash,* speed-recorded over three weekends, appeared in April 1977, it blew critics and fans away with its harmonic buzzsaw blasts of raw social and political protest. The band sounded like Woody Guthrie blown violently and passionately through a Marshall stack and of course, famously, in the first of many pioneering musical moves to come, dropped a cover of Junior Murvin's 'Police And Thieves' into the thick of the album, announcing an infatuation with reggae and their ambitions to be so much more than a punk rock group.

By the time the album had reached number 12 on the British album charts and sold over 100,000 copies, Terry Chimes (listed on the album sleeve as 'Tory Crimes') had left the band, citing irreconcilable political differences. After auditioning over 200 drummers, The Clash

hired Nicky 'Topper' Headon (born Bromley, Kent, May 30, 1955). With the classic Clash line-up solidified, the band's focus shifted to various disputes with CBS. The first concerned the label's refusal to release the album in the US (the decision would be reversed in 1979 once The Clash started making serious inroads into the American market), the second the company's move to pull 'Remote Control' from the album as a single without consulting the band. In response, they cut a barbed message to CBS, 'Complete Control', produced by Lee 'Scratch' Perry and released on 45 in September 1977.

Throughout that year, conflicts followed the band wherever they went. On tour in mid-1977, the police stopped and searched the members after a headlining show at the Civic Centre, St. Albans. Found in possession of Holiday Inn pillow cases, keys and towels – all souvenirs from the previous night's show in Newcastle – Strummer and Headon were charged with theft and arrested. After being released on £20 bail, a mere week later, Strummer was arrested again - this time for spray-painting the band's name on a wall in Camden. Needless to say, with their rebel/ outlaw image ever to the forefront, these run-ins with the police did nothing to hurt the band's punk credibility.

After a Jones-Strummer songwriting holiday in Jamaica, The Clash recorded their second album, *Give 'Em Enough Rope* in early 1978 with producer Sandy Pearlman (the distinctly un-punk one-time manager and producer of Blue Oyster Cult). In March 1978, to keep themselves in the public eye, they released the single 'Clash City Rockers', a catchy track every bit as self-aggrandising as Bo Diddley's 'Bo Diddley', that further mythologised their reputation as the 'last gang in town'. A month later, the band honed their political/social protest by headlining a huge Anti-Nazi League Carnival in London, organised by Rock Against Racism.

The band's first major step away from punk came in June 1978 when they released the punk-reggae hybrid 'White Man In Hammersmith Palais'. In one single, they built a musical bridge to a new sound. Meanwhile, Headon and Simonon were arrested for shooting at pigeons from the roof of their rehearsal studios after a passenger on a passing train had mistakenly thought the train was under attack and called the police. In court, Headon and Simonon were each charged with shooting at endangered pigeons, fined £30 and ordered to pay £700 compensation and £40 court costs. Barely had the dust settled on that incident, than Strummer was arrested again, after a gig at the Glasgow Apollo. Frustrated at battles between bouncers and fans throughout the show, Strummer smashed a lemonade bottle outside the venue and was arrested. When Simonon ran to his aide, he met the same fate. In court, the magistrate famously asked Strummer what the name of his 'group' was. He replied: "The Clash." The magistrate said: "How appropriate! £25."

Give 'Em Enough Rope appeared in autumn 1978 and entered the British album charts at number two. Concurrently, CBS's American counterpart, Epic Records, released the record in the US. That October, The Clash set off on the 'Sort It Out' tour, having sacked Bernie Rhodes and hired *Melody Maker* journalist (and Simonon's then girlfriend) Caroline Coon as their unofficial new manager. After releasing 'Tommy Gun' and 'English Civil War' as singles, the band flew out to begin their first American tour, dubbed Pearl Harbour '79. With Bo Diddley supporting, they gleefully opened each of the sold-out shows with 'I'm So Bored With The USA.' By the end of the tour, the band's love of American music and culture was at the forefront of their minds – as was cracking the American market. The first sign of this was the release of *The Cost Of Living* EP, spearheaded by their rousing cover version of Bobby Fuller Four's 1966 cover of The Crickets' 'I Fought The Law', a track that made public their passionate love of all things American. The EP arose from sessions intended to flesh out the soundtrack to a film they'd been involved with called

INTRODUCTION

Rudi Can't Fail (later released in 1980 as *Rude Boy*), a fictional documentary about an aimless young man who finds work as a roadie for The Clash.

In early 1979 the band began work on their third album, *London Calling*, produced by pill-popping, Sixties scenester Guy Stevens, who (allegedly) named Procol Harum and worked with Mick Jones' teenage heroes, Mott The Hoople. Recording enough material for a double album, a move that hardly thrilled CBS, a compromise saw *London Calling* released as a double album, but packaged in a single sleeve. The album in the can and armed with new management company Blackhill, the band took off for the US for 'The Clash Take The Fifth' tour. In New York, Mickey Gallagher, keyboards player with Ian Dury & The Blockheads, joined the band onstage and ended up playing on the rest of the tour. The tour was again a sell-out and the band undertook substantial radio and press interviews, another sign they were now pursuing mainstream success.

London Calling, released in December 1979, was unanimously hailed as an eclectic classic. Embracing rockabilly ('Brand New Cadillac'), jazz ('Jimmy Jazz'), reggae ('Guns Of Brixton', 'Rudie Can't Fail'), Motown ('Train In Vain'), brittle emotive pop ('Lost In The Supermarket'), clanging political/ social protest ('London Calling') and blistering rock 'n' roll ('Clampdown'), the album saw The Clash finally fuse their varied influences into one stupendous gumbo of an album. The iconic cover featured Pennie Smith's shot of Paul Simonon clubbing the stage with his bass and the artwork explicitly referenced Elvis Presley's iconic debut album. It sold well (though the album only peaked at number nine in the UK whereas *Give 'Em Enough Rope* had reached number two) and backed up by another American tour and a *Rolling Stone* magazine cover story, 'Train In Vain', which wasn't meant to make the final track listing (hence its non-appearance on the sleeve and label track listing), unexpectedly gave the band their first Top 30 American hit single in summer 1980.

In August 1980, The Clash released 'Bankrobber,' another reggae inspired single and the first fruits of a succession of studio/live collaborations with DJ Mikey Dread. Again, with Dread, the band headed for Jamaica, to lay down tracks for their fourth album.

The sessions didn't work out and with Dread, they flew on to New York's Electric Ladyland studio. In October 1980, to keep up American interest, Epic released *Black Market Clash*, a record which mopped up recent British B-sides and EP tracks. By the end of the year, The Clash were ready to unveil *Sandanista!*, a sprawling 36- track album which pushed the eclectic experimentations of *London Calling* too far. After yet another dispute with CBS, the album was released as a triple in a single sleeve for the standard price of a double album. In return, the band had to accept that they wouldn't see a penny in royalties until sales passed 200,000. When lead-off single, 'The Call Up' and the album were released at the end of 1980, both received lukewarm critical and commercial reaction. Overnight, The Clash was out in the cold. Two further singles – 'Hitsville UK' (January 1981) and the rap inspired 'The Magnificent Seven' (April 1981) - fared no better and from all points, it seemed that *Sandanista!*, had trashed all the positive momentum generated by *London Calling*

For the first time, individual members pursued interests outside the band. Strummer oversaw the release of a 101ers retrospective album, *Elgin Avenue Breakdown* and Mick Jones produced girlfriend Ellen Foley's album *Spirit Of St. Loui*s (she had guested as backing vocalist on *Sandanista!*) and co-produced Ian Hunter's *Short Back N'Sides*. Meanwhile, wanting to tour the US in support of *Sandanista!*, but finding that Epic were unwilling to finance such an outing for a record retailing at a low price, The Clash responded by setting up a seven-night residency at Bond's nightclub, near Times Square, NYC, in June 1981. These legendary shows set The Clash back on track in the US, as demand for tickets outstripped the venue's limited capacity. In the UK, increasingly inspired by The Sugarhill Gang, Grandmaster Flash and the Furious Five and other early 'old skool' rap artists breaking through to a mainstream audience, the rap-flavoured 'This is Radio Clash' was released as a single in November 1981. Again, it failed to even dent the Top 40 in the UK or the US, a message that fans were unwilling to let the band stray too far from what had made them great in the first place.

In response to the shaky situation, The Clash re-hired Bernie Rhodes as their manager and returned to Electric Ladyland in New York to self produce their fifth album, *Combat Rock* (initially

INTRODUCTION

slated to be called *Rat Patrol From Fort Bragg*). They had barely started when Topper Headon was busted for heroin possession at Heathrow airport in December 1981. He was fined £500 and given a conditional discharge. After a major polish job by producer Glyn Johns, the album was released in May 1982, a month after the single 'Know Your Rights'. *Combat Rock* was hailed as a return to form. Despite this, behind the scenes, the band was buckling under the pressure. Though the album was doing well, reaching number two on the British album chart, an entire 20-date UK tour had to be cancelled when Joe Strummer went AWOL. Eventually, he was located in Paris, where Rhodes persuaded Strumer to pick up the planned tour at a Dutch festival. No sooner was Strummer back in the fold, after the band travelled back to London Topper Headon announced he was leaving on account of "a difference of opinion over the political direction the group will be taking". Much later, it emerged that the others had in fact issued Topper with an ultimatum: quit heroin or quit the band. His dependence on the poppy was stronger.

The Clash's planned US tour went ahead in summer 1982, with original drummer Terry Chimes temporarily redrafted. The reenergised band ripped through the dates, with Strummer sporting a Mohican haircut, buoyed by news that *Combat Rock*'s first US single 'Should I Stay Or Should I Go?' had reached number 45. The album entered the American chart at the modest position of number 99 before climbing throughout the rest of the year, helped along by the release of 'Rock The Casbah'. It became the Clash's biggest hit while they were together as a band, reaching the US Top 10. The single was released in the UK in June 1982, followed by the double A-side, 'Should I Stay Or Should I Go?'/ 'Straight To Hell' in September. A month later, in a move that would have seen them publicly flogged by punk puritans in 1977, The Clash opened for The Who at New York's Shea Stadium. To equally massive audiences, the band played the Jamaica World Music Festival in November 1982 and the US festival in Los Angeles in May 1983.

With a formal replacement for Topper Headon– 23-year-old unknown Peter Howard - things seemed settled within the ranks and collective focus was on a sixth album. Over the summer, Strummer had an idea that the band should shoot a film around their native Ladbroke Grove. A collective effort, the black and white film, *Hell W10* would be

INTRODUCTION

the last project he and Mick Jones worked on as The Clash. In August 1983, Strummer and Simonon fired Jones, telling the press that the guitarist had "drifted apart from the original idea of The Clash". Jones refuted this statement, claiming he had been sacked without any discussion whatsoever. Late in 1983, The Clash announced a UK tour and at the beginning of 1984, a new line up, which beyond Strummer, Simonon and Howard, included two new guitarists: Vince White and Nick Sheppard, was unveiled. Though tickets sold out, the tour received a lukewarm response; Jones' absence was painfully apparent and noted by critics and fans alike. Without Topper and Jones, The Clash simply weren't The Clash anymore.

In May 1985, as the Clash Mk. II went out on a busking tour around northern England, Mick Jones was getting ready to unveil his new project, Big Audio Dynamite (BAD), which he'd put together with former Roxy club DJ and Clash filmmaker Don Letts. In autumn 1985, they unveiled their debut album, *This Is Big Audio Dynamite,* concurrent to the release of the new 'Clash' album: *Cut The Crap.* While *Cut The Crap* was deservedly slated, BAD's effort – a logical follow-on from the sound of 'The Magnificent Seven' and 'This Is Radio Clash' - was a success after the second single off the album, 'E=MC2', became a Top 30 hit in the UK. A hatchet burying of sorts occurred when Strummer co-wrote and co-produced BAD's second album, *No 11 Upping Street.* In mid-1987, BAD went out on a stadium tour, opening for U2. That same year, Topper Headon received an 18-month prison sentence for supplying heroin. He emerged clean in 1988, to start a new life, working as a mini-cab driver. (Topper's solo album, *Working Man*, was released in 1986.)

By the time the third BAD album, *Tighten Up Vol. 88*, appeared in 1988, Strummer was working in film with Alex Cox. He wrote songs for Cox's Sid Vicious biopic *Sid And Nancy*, appeared among a motley crew in *Straight To Hell* and travelled to Nicaragua to appear in *Walker*, for which he also wrote the score. Jones' good fortunes came to an abrupt end in 1988 when he caught chicken pox – potentially lethal when contracted as an adult. The illness quickly spiralled into pneumonia and then a life threatening coma. Faced with near death, it took Jones six months to convalesce. He returned in 1989, with a fourth BAD album, *Megatop Phoenix* followed by a fifth, *Kool Aid*, in 1990.

Paul Simonon had meanwhile formed Havana 3am with guitarist Gary Myrick and drummer Travis Williams, their debut album *Havana 3am* emerging in 1991 to little fanfare. Simonon had enjoyed a more favourable proxy success in 1990 when DJ Norman Cook (a.k.a. Fatboy Slim) scored a massive UK hit single with 'Dub Be Good To Me', a track released under the name Beats International, featuring a sample from 'Guns Of Brixton'. By this time, Strummer had penned the soundtrack to the film *Permanent Record*, appeared in Jim Jarmusch's *Mystery Train* and put together a new band, Latino Rockabilly War, with whom he recorded the overlooked 1989 album, *Earthquake Weather*.

The various solo activities of the Clash members were overshadowed in 1991 when Levi's approached CBS asking permission to use 'Should I Stay Or Should I Go?' to score a commercial for Levi's Red tab jeans. With Jones' blessing, the commercial went out and scored The Clash a whole new generation of fans. Jumping on the renewed interest, CBS re-issued 'Should I Stay Or Should I Go?' which gave the band their first number one single in the UK. Next came a reissue of 'Rock The Casbah' (sending much needed royalties Topper's way), followed by 'London Calling', a re-release of *The Story of The Clash Vol.1* (a compilation first put out in 1988), a new release called *Super Black Market Clash* (an expanded version of the US-only *Black Market Clash*) and late in 1991, *The Clash: The Singles*. Riding this renewed interest in The Clash, BAD, now onto their umpteenth line-up as BAD II, released a sixth album, *The Globe*.

INTRODUCTION 99

The early to mid-Nineties saw the ex-Clash members go through various changes. For Simonon, Havana 3am was a short lived affair, soon disbanded. He decided to return to his first love - painting - and has worked as an artist ever since. Mick Jones and BAD II went out on tour in 1992 and 1993 with U2 and in 1994, now known as Big Audio, released the album, *Higher Power*. The album *F-Punk* followed in 1995, then a world tour in 1996 and another album, *Entering A New Ride*, in 1997, which their label refused to release – leading Jones to drip-feed tracks to fans via the band's website, launched in 1998.

Strummer, meanwhile, had drifted into an artistic wilderness. After *Earthquake Weather* flopped, he entered into a stalemate with CBS/Sony who would neither release another solo record nor release him from his contract unless he could raise an unrealistic amount of money. Finding himself boxed into a corner, he produced The Pogues' *Hell's Ditch* in 1990, and jumped at a last-minute invitation to tour with them, as stand-in guitarist for Phil Chevron. In the late Nineties, Strumer found a backing band capable of matching his power and passion: The Mescaleros. Signed to American indie Hellcat/Epitaph, Strummer and The Mescaleros released two acclaimed albums: *Rock Art and the X-Ray Style* in 1999 and *Global-A Go Go* in 2001. In tandem with tours littered with old Clash songs and reggae covers, Strummer was back on track.

After years of rumours and offers regarding a Clash reformation and a steady stream of releases that maintained interest in the band – namely 1999's live album *From Here To Eternity* and Don Lett's Clash documentary *Westway To the World* - on November 16, 2002, when Strummer and The Mescaleros played a benefit for the London fire brigade, Mick Jones joined the band on stage at Acton Town Hall. It was the first time Strummer and Jones had shared a stage since 1983. Could a Clash reunification project seem possible? But just as Strummer was back in the groove again, fate intervened. On December 22, 2002, during work on the third Mescaleros album, *Streetcore*, Strummer died suddenly of a heart attack at his home in Broomfield, Somerset. A post-mortem gave the cause of a death as a congenital heart defect. He was only 50. As a fitting epitaph, in March 2003, The Clash were inducted into the Rock 'N' Roll Hall Of Fame, a confirmation of how broad their influence had been on bands like U2, Bad Brains, Rancid, Massive Attack, Green Day, No Doubt, Rage Against The Machine, Blink 182, The Afghan Whigs, The Minutemen, Manic Street Preachers, The Beastie Boys and The Libertines, to name but a few. To honour the band's induction, CBS released *The Essential Clash*, a new compilation and an accompanying DVD of promo videos and assorted rare film clips.

Since Strummer's untimely death and the posthumous release of *Streetcore* in 2003, Paul Simonon has continued to exhibit his artworks while Topper Headon leads a quiet existence. In 2004, CBS released a 25th anniversary edition of *London Calling,* including in the package the so-called 'lost' Vanilla Tapes, culled from the *London Calling* sessions. Mick Jones has kept the highest profile of the ex Clash members, producing both Libertines albums, as well as the debut album by Pete Doherty's Babyshambles. He has also been active with Carbon/Silicon, a new outfit put together with former London SS/Generation X/Sigue Sigue Sputnik maverick Tony James. Today sees The Clash arguably bigger than ever, their achievements looming large over the whole of the punk and post-punk landscape. Like The Velvet Underground, they might not have sold millions of records but their legacy remains tangible within modern music. As Joe Strummer once said, "We made it but in another way. We made it in the culture. We'll have our place. You don't have to worry about that. You don't have to worry about shallow rock mags that'll just blow away in the wind next week, man. You cannot take Creedence Clearwater or The Doors out of the culture. So it doesn't matter. Our place in the culture will probably be even-steven with a lot of people who fill stadiums."

INTRODUCTION

Life Before The Clash

Mick Jones

"I grew up in Brixton and went to school there." **2005**

"My parents split up when I was eight. It was a big thing." 2005

"Then I moved as an early teenager to West London with my gran, where she brought me up.**"**

2005

"I first saw The New York Dolls opening for Rod Stewart & The Faces, who were one of the groups I used to follow around the country when I was 12 and 13. Me and my friends would sneak onto the trains. We'd go to see Mott The Hoople, Ziggy Stardust & The Spiders from Mars, Humble Pie. I made my mind up around then that I was going to be in a group. The choices back then were football or pop music. I didn't fancy boxing." 1995

"I liked all the groups that were around in the Sixties. I started following a band called Mott The Hoople up and down the country. I would follow this group and just sleep on the steps of the town hall or something, and then go back the next day. So I knew very early on that I wanted to be in a band." **2000**

"Once I'd decided to be a guitarist, I spent a couple of years in my bedroom playing along with records.**"** 2005

"My main influences are Mott The Hoople, The Kinks and The Stones.**"** 1977

"*The Harder They Come, Mean Streets, Lafayette,* **with Jack Hawkins about the American War of Independence.** *Les Enfants Terribles* **by Jean Cocteau."**

ON HIS FAVOURITE FILMS, 1977

"I only ever wanted to be in a band, so I went to art school in Hammersmith. I thought that was the traditional route you took.**"** 2005

"Before The Clash, Tony James and I used to put adverts in the music papers about every week, looking for anybody into The Stooges or the [New York] Dolls. There was a cafe around the corner where we had all our records on the jukebox, and we used to meet the people who answered our ad there. We'd play them some records and sort of check them out and if they weren't complete dorks, we'd take them to a little rehearsal studio that we had nearby." ON THE MANY LINE-UPS OF LONDON SS, 1995

"I was working at the social security. SS, you see.**"**

ON NAMING LONDON SS, 2005

"Bernie [Rhodes, unofficial manager of London SS] was mates with Malcolm McLaren so we were aware of the Sex Pistols and they were aware of us." ON EMERGING PUNK SCENE IN LONDON, 2005

LIFE BEFORE THE CLASH

Joe Strummer

"I grew up in Ankara. It's the capital of Turkey. My father was in the foreign office. I was born there. I also have Armenian blood. And Scottish. I grew up eighteen months in Turkey, eighteen months in Cairo, two years in Mexico, two years in West Germany, then I went to boarding school in Epsom and I visited my parents in Tehran for five years and then Malawi for a few years and then went to art school, dropped out, became a bum." 1988

"I wasn't close to my parents because when I was eight years old I was sent to a boarding school, where I spent nine years. I saw my father once a year between the ages of nine to twelve, then twice a year from then on." 2001

"I was in boarding school, locked up really good for nine years and all of a sudden you're staying at a hostel in Battersea, with no one to say what to do, where to go. It was 1970 and there was drink and drugs and by the end we were doing acid and I never went near art school."

1988

"Well, I started playing music around '73. I'd tried everything else and I couldn't find anything I wanted to do or anywhere to be. So I got into music because it seemed like the best thing around. You could say it was the thing that had the least laws and restrictions about it." 1981

"Living in Wales was like a rock and roll school for me. I had some mates at Newport Art College and crashed with them. Then I got a job at a cemetery and started playing in the art college rock band. We did gigs in some of the roughest clubs in the Valleys and had the locals shouting abuse and chucking things at us, the bastards! But they were honestly great times." 2002

"When I was sixteen, *Trout Mask Replica* was the only record I listened to for a year." 1978

"We blagged a gig in Bristol and we couldn't really play so a kind of near riot ensued and we had to leg it. That's when the Vultures broke up." ON THE BREAK UP OF HIS FIRST BAND, THE VULTURES (FORMERLY FLAMING YOUTH), 2000

"Dr. Feelgood were the undisputed kings of that scene. We were the latecomers, more like the dirty cousins, because we were squat-rockers and a bit younger and a bit more incapable. We didn't know our chops as well. Eventually we got skilled enough to be probably the second-best rhythm and blues group in West London after Feelgood, but it took a year and a half to get there. The thrill of discovering old blues numbers and playing them to people and making them groove. To us it was new and exciting." ON HIS FIRST SERIOUS BAND, THE 101ERS, 2000

"Eventually Allan Jones from *Melody Maker* who I'd known from Newport, I got him to come down to The Pig Dog, hoping that we'd get a bit of press and he wrote four lines at the bottom of their gossip column. Me and Big John Cassell (saxophone player) took this four lines down to the Elgin pub (on Ladbroke Grove) and we showed it to the landlord and then he read it and said, 'Right lads then, I'll give you ten pounds.' That's when we got on to the circuit." ON THE 101ERS FIRST BREAK, 1988

LIFE BEFORE THE CLASH

❝I went out in the crowd which was fairly sparse. And I saw the future, with a snotty handkerchief, right in front of me. It was immediately clear. Pub rock was, 'Hello, you bunch of drunks, I'm gonna play these boogies and I hope you like them.' The Sex Pistols came out that Tuesday evening and their attitude was, 'Here's our tunes, and we couldn't give a flying fuck whether you like them or not. In fact, we're gonna play them even if you fucking hate them.' They were a really firing live unit. There was something magical about Steve Jones' guitar ability, like the sound of ten guys playing the guitar. You had Rotten's amazing stage presence and Matlock's a fantastic bass player, as good as Paul McCartney and then Paul Cook hammering. No smoke or mirrors needed.❞

ON SEEING THE SEX PISTOLS OPEN FOR
THE 101ERS IN APRIL 1976, 2000

❝Punk hit London and suddenly, which side of the line were you on? There was the Pistols and the people walking around with them: alright, there was only ten of them, but it was starting to mushroom and we were on the very bottom rung, living in the squats, where ideas come in very quickly. There were still a lot of hippies about, so you were either against punks or with them. You couldn't stand around saying, 'Well, I'm not sure.' So the 101ers really had to fall apart because most of the group were against punks and I was with them.❞ **2000**

Hey Joe

"One day, I just remember that I went out to West London. We met this guy named Mick Jones, known as 'Rock and Roll Mick' at the time. We really became instant fast friends. He said, 'Keith, what do you want to do?' I said, 'All I know is I want to form a band.' I told him that I was fucking great on guitar. I had no qualms about saying it. I was just 16."

KEITH LEVENE, 2001

"I met Mick Jones at the tail end of 1975, early 1976. Mick had about five songs at that time but until I came along and added my bit to it and added my sound to it, they sounded like shit." **KEITH LEVENE, 2002**

"You have to understand that Bernie Rhodes was integral to the birth of The Clash." PAUL SIMONON, 2004

"Bernie Rhodes was competing with Malcolm McLaren. He was going, 'This is the hippest scene you're ever going to be on.' And this was before we had a band or we had a name or we had a bass player." **KEITH LEVENE, 2002**

HEY JOE

" This guy that I knew was a drummer, and he told me, 'Come to art college, it's a dawdle, and you don't have to do anything really.' And he got in, and he was walking through Notting Hill Gate one day and these two guys stopped him and said, 'Are you a drummer?' He says, 'Yeah,' and they says, 'Well come down to this audition,' and I tagged along with him. And when I arrived I was confronted with Mick Jones, Brian James, Tony James and various blokes waiting for their turn to be the drummer. And Mick or one of them, piped up, 'Are you a singer?' I said, 'No, I'm not.' They said, 'Do you wanna have a go?' So I had to give it a go. There was a guy in the corner, who was Bernie Rhodes, and my first words to him were, 'Are you their manager?' And he was like: 'Why? What's it to you?' So I was like, 'Fair enough.' And then a couple of days later he told Mick to sack his group and get a group together with me. " PAUL SIMONON, 1999

" Bernard Rhodes thought there was a grittiness about me that might be a good ingredient. " **PAUL SIMONON, 2002**

" Mick said, "I've got an idea for this guy. He comes across a bit thick but he's really good. He's really good looking and he's an artist.' That was Paul Simonon. So I met Paul one day and I really liked him. Paul moves in at the squat at Davis Road, so I really get to know him and he's just like this big kid but he's really hard too. He's the real thing. " KEITH LEVENE, 2002

" To simplify it for myself, I painted the notes on the neck of the guitar. So if Mick said, 'This song starts in D and then it's G and then it's F,' I had it all there. I pretty much coloured the whole fretboard in. And after learning parrot fashion, it was only a matter of time before I could take the letters off. "

PAUL SIMONON, ON LEARNING THE BASS, 1999

" When I met Mick, he was into rock 'n' roll completely. I liked David Bowie but the reggae thing was more important. What changed things was when we got Joe in the group. He was into Bo Diddley, Woody Guthrie and Bob Marley. He was the part-hippie of the group. " PAUL SIMONON, 2005

"After rehearsals with just me and Mick and whoever we could find really to play the drums, and we had Keith Levene with us, we were just trying to build the group up and the Pistols were just starting to do their shows at that time, and it was only later when we saw Strummer in The 101ers that we thought, 'We'll nick him for our group.' And we did and that was the start of The Clash, really. Once we had Joe on board it all started to come together.**"** **PAUL SIMONON, 1999**

"There were, like, dogs walking across stage, hippy blokes wandering around, but in the middle of all this, this bloke, just giving it really serious attitude with a guitar. We were looking for a singer and there he was."

PAUL SIMONON, ON SEEING JOE STRUMMER PLAYING WITH THE 101ERS, 2002

"So we were getting The Clash together and I was feeling a bit embarrassed about these guys. We had this singer who was this real Mick Jagger imitation. Me and Bernard Rhodes went off to a 101ers gig one night and talked Joe Strummer into coming over to my squat in Shepherd's Bush. I was playing guitar with him and playing some 101ers tunes. He went, 'Hey man, I just love you and I love the way you play guitar.' So I said, 'Will you do it?' He said, 'Yeah,' and we got him in The Clash.**"** **KEITH LEVENE, 2001**

"I don't like your group but we think you're great."

WHAT MICK JONES SAID WHEN HE FIRST MET JOE STRUMMER, 1976

HEY JOE

"At the 100 Club, Bernie Rhodes comes up to me and says, 'You're in The 101ers, give me your number, I've got to call you about something.' We had a squat in Orsett Terrace. A few nights later at the Golden Lion Pub, Fulham Broadway, Bernie came down with Keith Levene. The 101ers were going, 'Who's this?' I went outside to talk to Bernie. We were hanging out and Bernie gave me an ultimatum and said, 'Look, I'll give you 24 hours, I've got to go on this thing, so you're in or you're out, dial me in 24 hours.' So I thought about it all night and I thought about it all day and I rang him and I just said, 'I'm in.' And that was before meeting Mick and Paul. What really sold me was Keith Levene, in those days, people looked really boring, and Keith looked different." **JOE STRUMMER, 1978**

"**They were already kind of doing it: Simmo, Keith Levene and Mick Jones and what they really lacked was someone to give it a front. A front guy or a lyric writer. They were like a jigsaw waiting for the piece to fall in.**" JOE STRUMMER, 2002

"You couldn't understand a word he was fucking saying, he had terrible teeth, but he'd fucking move and he'd be like this big pile of sweat." **KEITH LEVENE, ON JOE STRUMMER, 2002**

"**He went, 'God I love the way you play guitar, man, you just play anything. I love the way you make things up.' And we did 'Keys To Your Heart' and I'm singing it with him and he's going, 'Oh I fucking love you!' And he grabbed me and he said, 'I'll do it, I'll do it, I'm gonna do it, I'm gonna do it. What's the band called?' I said, 'I don't know but I know one thing: we've got a fucking killer singer.'**" KEITH LEVENE ON FIRST TIME PLAYING WITH JOE STRUMMER, 2002

"Bernie Rhodes said, 'I want you to come along and meet the other two.' So I went along and I met Paul and Mick and I kind of decided there and then to throw my lot in. The 101ers had really disintegrated anyway." **JOE STRUMMER, 2002**

Early Chemistry

"Write about things that affect you." BERNIE RHODES, 1976

"I was changing up my vibe so I dumped everything that I had in order to go forward. Mick had parts of songs, one which became 'I'm So Bored With The USA' and another which we eventually recorded as a B-side '1-2 Crush On You'. We took pieces of 'Jail Guitar Doors' which I had from The 101ers and we rewrote a different verse. But mostly it was kind of let's make it new.**"**

JOE STRUMMER, 2002

"I would consider myself mainly a lyric guy." JOE STRUMMER, 2002

"Mick said, here's one of mine – it's called 'I'm So Bored With The USA' and I said, 'Great title!' So I wrote it on a piece of paper to make a note of it. He went, 'No, no – I'm so bored with you.' I went, 'No this is better.' He went, 'No, no it's about my girlfriend.' I went, 'Not any more!'**"**

JOE STRUMMER, ON WRITING 'I'M SO BORED WITH THE USA', 2002

"'I'm So Bored With The USA' was 'I'm So Bored With You' until Joe added the 'S' and the A." MICK JONES, 1995

"I definitely remember playing along with it. Just after we'd formed, when we were practising.**"**

JOE STRUMMER ON BEING INFLUENCED BY THE RAMONES' DEBUT ALBUM, 2002

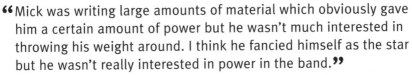

"Me and Sid Vicious we used to hang out together and it was Dee Dee Ramone that set the standard for me and for Sid as well. And we adopted accordingly."

PAUL SIMONON, 1999

"Mick was writing large amounts of material which obviously gave him a certain amount of power but he wasn't much interested in throwing his weight around. I think he fancied himself as the star but he wasn't really interested in power in the band."

TERRY CHIMES, 2003

"The best place you could hear bass was on the reggae records and when I got more in control of the instrument, I was able to bring that into the groove as an influence. The good thing about reggae for me was that they always had something to say. Bernie had essentially said to Joe, 'Don't write about your girlfriend or whatever, write about things that affect you.' And we already had the blueprint - reggae. But we didn't want to be a reggae group. It was about making our own music rather than just slavishly copying reggae. But there was a hint of it, a colour."

PAUL SIMONON, 1999

"Bernie Rhodes was really important to the whole sound. He was important on all levels of contribution, to when we started."

MICK JONES, 2000

"Joe was shocked I'd only been playing a few months. But he was relieved I had a bit of passion, the way I threw the guitar around. There was a connection: I had no baggage musically and Joe chucked his away when he joined The Clash. It was like, 'We're starting fresh. We're gonna create a new world!' How naïve. But you have that attitude when you're that age. Me and Joe, we were always at ease. We were still really close friends. He always treated me as his younger brother." PAUL SIMONON, 2003

EARLY CHEMISTRY

"We were all on speed. Not that we could afford it that much, but our drug intake was financially limited. Our idea of a good time was scoring a lump of dope the size of four match heads. Now and then we'd get some blues or a little bit of sulphate but Keith was much more pro on speed, sometimes I'd see him with a plastic bag of resiny balls, speed in very pure form.**"** JOE STRUMMER, 1988

**"We sort of nicked Paul Simonon from an art college.
We said, 'Throw those old paintbrushes away! Look, here's
a bass guitar.'"** JOE STRUMMER, 1997

"After rehearsals we'd sit down and ask each other what we wanted out of it and there's that famous line about Terry Chimes replying, 'I want a Lamborghini,' which was fine for him. But, yeah, we cross-referenced with each other, and asked, 'Where are we going? What makes this band different?,' rather than, 'Let's all get drunk, pull birds and play guitars and that's it.' We wanted more depth, a more human approach.**"** PAUL SIMONON, 2004

EARLY CHEMISTRY

Early Days Of The Clash

❝For about a weekend we were called The Psychotic Negatives, then we were the Weak Heart Drops, after a lyric in a Big Youth record. Then Paul thought of the name The Clash.❞

JOE STRUMMER, ON NAMING THE BAND, 1988

❝Paul thought the name The Clash was quite a good idea, that it sort of represented what had happened among us and what we were doing within the scene. Another reason they liked it was 'cos it came up a lot. There was a clash in the situation or the clash over benefits raises or the clash over pensions.❞ **KEITH LEVENE, 2002**

❝I've got one thing to say about being the bass player. I didn't want the role of being Entwistle or Bill Wyman, stuck in the background. That's too depressing and if that was what I'd been offered with The Clash I would've turned it down. Maybe that's the nature of the job or has been in the past; the bass player as the one that held the fort, so to speak, along with the drummer, letting everybody else go lunatic. But, you know, why can't we all be lunatics?❞ PAUL SIMONON, 1999

❝I'd grown up listening to John Bonham so I wanted to be the hardest hitting rock drummer in the world. I wanted to really splat that beat down hard and that kind of fitted The Clash's material.❞

TERRY CHIMES, 2002

❝It was great. We made a few screw-ups. That was the first time Simmo was on stage and so forth. We actually managed to play the tunes. It was highly entertaining.❞

JOE STRUMMER, ON THE FIRST GIG SUPPORTING THE SEX PISTOLS
ON JULY 4, 1976 AT THE BLACK SWAN, SHEFFIELD, 2002

"We'd go and hang out up there (on the balcony of Mick Jones' grandmother's 18th floor flat overlooking the Westway), just lean on the rail and look down across where the Westway crosses over Royal Oak. We'd spend night after night up there and one night I went home to our squat on Orsett Terrace and just sat down and wrote it, whispering because my girlfriend was asleep.**"**

JOE STRUMMER ON WRITING
'LONDON'S BURNING', 2002

"The Clash are the kind of garage band who should speedily be returned to their garage, preferably with the motor running."

CHARLES SHAAR MURRAY OF *NME*,
REVIEWING THE BAND'S PERFORMANCE
ON A PUNK BILL AT THE SCREEN ON THE
GREEN, ISLINGTON, AUGUST, 1976

"'White Riot' was a call to arms really. Joe wrote it after the Notting Hill Carnival riot in 1976. Me and him were there when it all kicked off under the Westway. It started with paper cups, then next minute we were running around with bricks and trying to set cars on fire. I remember we went back to the squat where Sid Vicious was. He'd missed it all so he wanted us to take him back down that night and see the riot. So we was walking up Tavistock Road with Sid when this bloke stopped us and said, 'I wouldn't go up there if you wanna keep your life.' At that point, we realised it might be wise to turn back!**"** PAUL SIMONON, 2003

"Songs like 'White Riot' were written walking along the street in my head." JOE STRUMMER, 1978

EARLY DAYS OF THE CLASH

❝I did a lot of learning in public. I just pretended I was Pete Townshend and jumped around a lot.**❞ PAUL SIMONON, 2002**

❝It's always said Keith got thrown out of The Clash because of drugs! That's bollocks! The reason I left the Clash was because I got too depressed being in the band. They were embarrassing. They were just too lame for me. I'd start turning up at rehearsals and I was really being a miserable git. I wasn't saying anything, just playing the numbers fine. Things would happen when Mick wasn't there where we'd work out something of mine. Then the next rehearsal, we'd get there and it would be a completely different version. That different version could have been another song. We could have kept the idea I worked on, kept what they worked on and called it something else. There seemed to be a my way/your way of doing things. At the same time, they suddenly came up with this idea for 'White Riot'. I said, 'I'm not fucking singing 'White Riot' – you're joking!'❞

KEITH LEVENE, 2001

❝Keith began to lose interest and I lost my temper with him when he rang up and we were doing 'White Riot'. He said, 'What are you working on? The 'White Riot' tune? Well there's no need for me to come up then, is there?' I said, 'Make that never, man.' Bernie was quite shocked when he arrived at rehearsals and I'd sacked him. Mick and Keith had a competition about who was going to be the lead guitar player, so Mick was quite pleased that Keith was sacked.❞ JOE STRUMMER, 1988

❝When it came to drugs, yeah, we were doing a bit of speed. I could handle my comedowns but Joe used to have terrible comedowns. But it wasn't about drugs. It was about, I found The Clash to be a lame punk rock band. They weren't the band I wanted them to be. I didn't like the clothes they wore! I didn't like the fucking outfits. I liked Bernard. I didn't like the tunes. I didn't like any of the fucking tunes on the first album, even the one I wrote: 'What's My Name'. It wasn't hard enough. So we had this little vote very quickly. Mick said, 'I want him out.' Joe said, 'I want him out.' Paul just went with the flow of the band. So I was out. Terry Chimes, for some reason, didn't get a vote. And that was it. I was out, I was gone.❞ KEITH LEVENE, 2001

❝After Keith left we sat down and played all the stuff without him and thought, 'Well, actually, we can do this and it's less complicated with less people.'❞ TERRY CHIMES, 2002

❝Terry wanted to join a pop group and get a Lamborghini, your average suburban kid's dream, right? And we used to have discussions, we were quite rigorous and when he said this about the Lamborghini, it was heresy. We were laughing and jeering at him and he took it very seriously and one day he just didn't show up for rehearsals. He phoned up and said he quit. But he was cool enough to come and do the album with us, cos we'd rehearsed the numbers with him.❞

JOE STRUMMER, ON TERRY CHIMES' QUITTING THE BAND THEN AGREEING TO STAY ON TO CUT DEMOS AND THE DEBUT ALBUM, 1988

EARLY DAYS OF THE CLASH

On The Anarchy
Tour With The
Sex Pistols
1976

"You would look at the stage and it was just twinkling in broken glass. And the drummer's got his cymbals turned flat on to protect himself. That's why we ran around onstage so much, 'cause we were ducking the bottles.**"** PAUL SIMONON, 2003

"I just thought of all the hours I've stood up there being spat at. It's horrible. When it dries on your shirt, it makes it go crusty. And you can't help getting it in your mouth. And then some lands on the fretboard of the guitar and you haven't noticed and slide your hand up there." JOE STRUMMER, ON ALL THAT SPIT, 1978

"I learned there's no romance in being on the road." MICK JONES, 1978

"That's the difference between us and the Pistols. I think we're more optimistic. The Pistols said there was no future and we say there is a future. But I've got great respect for the Pistols. They're my favourite group. People tried to make out there was a feud between us but that's rubbish. The clever thing for me to do now would be to attack the Pistols. That would make us popular with some people over here but the Pistols were great." MICK JONES, 1978

"All that business on the Pistols tour! I hated it. I HATED it. It was the Pistols time. We were in the background. The first few nights were terrible. We were just locked up in the hotel room with the Pistols doing nothing. And yet for me it was great too. We had the

coach and we had the hotels and we had something to do – even though they didn't let us do it that often. We did it about eight times. It was good fun. But when I got back to London on Christmas Eve I felt awful. I was really destroyed because after a few days you get used to eating. We were eating Holiday Inn rubbish but it was two meals a day and that. And when I got off the coach we had no money and it was just awful. I felt twice as hungry as I'd ever felt before. I had nowhere to live and I remember walking away from the coach deliberately not putting on my woolly jumper. I walked all the way up Tottenham Court Road and it was really cold but I wanted to get as cold and as miserable as I could. Christmas was here and me and Micky Foote, our soundman, had our little bags in our hands and it just felt like the worst thing in the world that the tour had ended. I wanted it to go on and on. The coach had been like home in a way and I didn't want to get off it. **"**

JOE STRUMMER, ON COMING OFF THE ANARCHY TOUR, 1978

ON THE ANARCHY TOUR WITH THE SEX PISTOLS 1976 **"**

On Image &Ideas

"First and foremost it was always a group. Our main concept was that everyone should move. All action, no fucking lazing about. No one riding on anyone's back. Everyone working full-tilt. It's much better to have a group working full-tilt. It's a real group." JOE STRUMMER, 1978

"We'd get hold of second-hand Sixties suits nobody wanted. You got a short haircut and straight trousers with a bit of Jackson Pollock splattered on." **PAUL SIMONON, 2002**

"Once at a rehearsal, Joe got a piece of chalk and drew a line on the floor and said, 'On this side is the musicians and on this side are the entertainers.' So me and Joe were on one side and Mick and Topper on the other. It was like, 'Who cares about a few wrong notes? We want to see some people jumping around, we wanna see some excitement, we wanna be entertained, not us all standing dead still getting it all right. You may as well listen to the record.'" PAUL SIMONON, 1999

"This stuff about fans staying in our hotel rooms and coming backstage is very important – the responsibility is to the fans, not only to keep in touch but also to show that we do care and I believe that this group cares more than any other in the country. I don't know any other group that in its soul cares as much as The Clash. Our idea was not to live out their fantasies for them but to show them that they could live out their own fantasies." **MICK JONES, 1978**

ON IMAGE & IDEAS

"Clothes were where my aesthetic instincts came out then. They helped make the group accessible." PAUL SIMONON, 2002

"We had to throw all those boring, ridiculous Emerson Lake & Palmer people out of a job. Some of the old duffers changed their tune, like The Rolling Stones. We lit a fire under their backsides, I can tell you that." JOE STRUMMER, 1984

"When we started out as young men with drainpipe trousers, the rest of the world was flared. We were an instant target. You got blokes chucking bottles at our concerts who didn't want anything to do with the idea of punk."

PAUL SIMONON, 2002

"The look was a really important part of it to me. The interesting groups that were around just before punk - The New York Dolls, Stooges, MC5, each had a great sounding guitarist who looked great and had a great looking guitar. I eventually got a Les Paul Junior because that's what Johnny Thunders played." MICK JONES, 1995

"It's great in this neighbourhood. There's this black family next door and really early in the morning they play all this dub. I don't even need to put anything on to listen to when I'm getting up."
PAUL SIMONON, ON LIVING IN LADBROKE GROVE AND HOW IT INFLUENCED
THE CLASH MUSICALLY, 1979

"Bernie Rhodes was very conscientious about designing how covers would look. He put a lot of effort into designing the look of the covers and artwork and flyers." JOE STRUMMER, 2002

Signing To CBS

" Guy Stevens produced our original demos. Just before we signed to CBS we were supposed to sign to Polydor and they paid for some demos. We went to a studio and Guy was producing but it never worked out. Then the next thing we signed to CBS anyway. " MICK JONES, 2004

" Punk died the day The Clash signed to CBS. "

MARK PERRY, SNIFFIN' GLUE, 1977

" Our defence would be that it helped make punk a worldwide concern. When we signed, people went, 'My god! That means it's serious!' We weren't thinking like cool music heads. We were insane idiots, which helped make our music better. "

JOE STRUMMER, 1999

" They probably saw us as a deductible throwaway, a few grand on that group, who knows what might happen, better get one of them punk groups before they all run out – that kind of vibe. We were in the cheapest studio. I got the feeling they were going to spend the price of an egg sandwich on us. " **JOE STRUMMER, 2002**

SIGNING TO CBS

The Clash
1977

"They did all look pretty intimidating. They were wearing all the gear in the studio. This was not an act. The bondage trousers. Mick had that shirt with 'Hate and War' painted on the back. There was a lot of gobbing on the floor and a bit of rowdiness.**"**

SIMON HUMPHREY, SOUND ENGINEER, CBS STUDIOS, WHITFIELD STREET, LONDON, REFLECTING ON THE SESSIONS FOR THE DEBUT ALBUM, 2002

"I do remember. Well, I don't not remember making it. We did it very fast, in a matter of three or four weekends from start to end, including everything and we mixed it with our regular sound guy, Mickey Foote. We didn't really know anything about production at that time. It was like, 'Have you ever heard of balancing?'**"** MICK JONES, 2005

"The first album was really a case of bashing out the live set in a studio. The only song that sounded very different from what we played live was 'Police And Thieves'. We began experimenting with harmonies, realising we could do overdubs and all those kinds of things." TERRY CHIMES, 2003

"We certainly have a sense of humour, a really highly developed one, amongst ourselves. A lot of things made us fall about laughing, people took very serious. Some of the words on that first album: me and Mick laughed till we cried." **JOE STRUMMER, 1978**

"When we wrote 'White Riot' and all that about Sten guns in Knightsbridge and knives in W11, we imagined what was gonna hit on us. I imagined having a knife pointed at me, right? I imagined Sten guns in Knightsbridge pointed at me. But people took it to mean we had them and we were pointing them at other people. That was a song written about the future. I thought the future was gonna do us in. I really did." JOE STRUMMER, 1979

"Reggae was punk's other chosen music. There weren't enough good punk records and so DJ's used to supplement them with what was happening on the reggae scene. One of the main DJ's was Don Letts, who was in the first Big Audio Dynamite. He used to turn everybody on to new records from Jamaica. Also, where we grew up in Brixton, there was a big West Indian population. There was bluebeat and ska, before reggae. We grew up around that music as well. In the way that the Stones used to cover the latest R & B hits, when they started, the Clash did 'Police And Thieves.' It was the latest hit of that summer. That's how we ended up doing it. We weren't trying to do reggae. We were trying to do our approximation, where we were coming from. It turned out differently. It wasn't like the Police doing a wet reggae thing." **MICK JONES, 1995**

THE CLASH 1977

THE CLASH *Talking*

❝My favourite song off that first album would have to
be 'Garageland.' Great fun to play live. I love the lyrics
and the sentiment but more than anything I just love the sound.
We never thought it was going to be an anthem because we never
thought about the future. We were very much a band of now.
I mean we thought we were going to be famous but we never
really considered the implications of that. I was always the one
who thought the punk 'sell-out' thing was nonsense anyway.
You have to have a record label, you have to have money coming
in. I was a realist, whereas the others used to fight against it.
We used to argue all the time about that stuff.❞ TERRY CHIMES, 2003

❝To me, 'Garageland' almost, I dunno, it puts an exclamation mark
at the end of the punk period. I mean, we signed to the record
company and like the song says, 'My mates have got new boots,'
that's what it was like.❞ **PAUL SIMONON, 2003**

"It's funny what people hear sometimes. Like this one bloke thought for months that we were singing, 'Quite Right,' instead of, 'White Riot!'"

MICK JONES, 1977

"There was a feeling of every second you spend in the studio you're going to have to pay back later." JOE STRUMMER, 2002

"The main problem I had with them was getting them to turn up together."

SIMON HUMPHREY, 2002

"Any guitar of note on the record is Jonesy." JOE STRUMMER, 2002

"We were jumping up and down. We knew that we'd brought something to the party. It wasn't like a slavish white man's xerox of some riff. It was like: Give us your riff and we'll drive it around London. Scratch Perry liked it."

JOE STRUMMER ON 'POLICE AND THIEVES' 2002

"They really knew how to be photographed and they gave you the stillness that you needed and the respect that you needed and the attention. They were a photographer's dream."

KATE SIMON, PHOTOGRAPHER OF THE ALBUM COVER SHOT, 2002

THE CLASH 1977

Enter Topper

"I first played drums when I was thirteen. I was working at the butchers, cleaning up and I saved the money to buy a kit for £30."

TOPPER HEADON, 1977

"I used to steal a lot and run with a gang.**" TOPPER HEADON, 1979**

"I wasn't into reggae until I joined The Clash. All Paul played on the tour bus was reggae. I remember a lot of Prince Far–I. I suddenly started thinking, 'Hmmm, that's quite good.'"

TOPPER HEADON, 2005

"I can relate to The Clash on a political level. I've been through the unemployment bit. I've been made to take jobs that I didn't want at all. I knew Mick Jones from about a year and a half ago. For a week, I played with his band, The London SS, when Brian James of The Damned and Tony James of Generation X were in it too. Then I didn't see him for ages until I bumped into him at The Kinks concert at the Rainbow last month. I'd never seen them play but I was really excited as soon as I did. They are incredible. I really wanted to join. They are by far the best band in the country.**" TOPPER HEADON, 1977**

On Getting Arrested

"It was boring. Irritating! Spending the night in jail!"

JOE STRUMMER, 1977

ON GETTING ARRESTED

Complete Control

❝When I got involved with that record, most of it was already done. I liked The Clash, they were nice boys. I taught them to turn down their guitars in the studio. They were loud man, loud!❞

LEE 'SCRATCH' PERRY ON HIS INVOLVEMENT WITH PRODUCING 'COMPLETE CONTROL', 1984

❝**The chaos of Lee Scratch Perry was absolutely what The Clash loved.**❞ CAROLINE COON, 2005

❝We was on tour and 'Remote Control' was put out behind our backs. We were angry, yeah, but 'Complete Control' was funny as hell.❞ **PAUL SIMONON, 2003**

❝**He's a wild guy. He was shit hot. He nearly blew the control room up trying to get Paul a bass sound.**❞

MICKEY FOOTE ON LEE 'SCRATCH' PERRY, 2004

❝We went to Amsterdam for the first time and it was like this circus around us, which was so amusing. We were just trying to make sense of it all. At that point it was the only non-reggae record Lee Perry had made.❞ **MICK JONES, 2003**

❝**It's a bit difficult for me to talk about Lee Perry because by the time he was there I had really bad flu. I recorded my bass part, only saw him for half an hour then had to go and lie down. Missed the whole thing.**❞ PAUL SIMONON, 2003

The Songwriting Holiday In Jamaica

❝We wanted to get away for a couple of weeks and we couldn't go to Paris because we know too many girls there and would have got distracted. So I said, 'What about Jamaica?' And Bernie (Rhodes) said no. But a week or so later, he came in with the plane tickets. We went there to get away from everything and wrote the new album but it was a lonely time for me and Mick. We didn't know anybody and you have to go everywhere in taxis, you can't just walk about. Two white blokes, they'd knife you. We couldn't afford taxis at the time. It wasn't until the end we felt relaxed. I'd like to go sometime for about six months.❞

JOE STRUMMER, 1978

❝Me and Joe wrote 'Safe European Home' in Jamaica. We were way out of our depth to tell you the truth. Obviously Paul Simonon was really pissed off because he didn't get to go. It wasn't our fault. Bernie Rhodes said, 'You gotta write a record so go and have a holiday somewhere.' We didn't take him seriously because he was always saying things like that.❞ MICK JONES, 2003

THE SONGWRITING HOLIDAY IN JAMAICA ❞❞

"If you're a white band and you want to use Channel One Studio, they think you're rich, which you are, really, compared to them hanging about there. And you've got to bounce up the local population, you know? We didn't have anything to give them, so we had to leave. It's really tough down there now. There's not really a lot of money about." **JOE STRUMMER, 1981**

"When me and Joe went to Jamaica we spent a whole day in this cab trying to find his [Lee Perry's] Black Ark studio. We knew he had this picture of us and it was the only band that wasn't a reggae band on his wall. But we got totally lost and never found it." MICK JONES, 2003

White Man In Hammersmith Palais

"All over the world people are oppressed and in London there were the dreads and there were the punks and we had an alliance. England is a very repressive country. Immigrants were treated badly. So these people had a sense of pride and dignity, and when we went into their concerts, where we should have had the grace to have left them alone, they didn't jump us, they didn't stomp us, they didn't beat the seven shades of you know what out of us. They understood that maybe we needed a drop of this roots culture. And 'White Man in Hammersmith Palais' is a song that was going through my mind while I was standing in the middle of the Hammersmith Palais in a sea of thousands of rastas and dreads and natty rebels. That song was trying to say something realistic."
JOE STRUMMER ON THE STORY BEHIND
'WHITE MAN IN HAMMERSMITH PALAIS,' 1981

"**What I loved about The Clash, they weren't apprehensive about tackling reggae.**" DON LETTS, 2005

"It's like a couple of songs in one. Same with 'Complete Control' and 'Clash City Rockers.' They're almost like mini-operas. It's got that reggae element but it's also a rock song. It's not a punk song but then again it is. It's a combination of all those elements."
PAUL SIMONON, 2003

"**Hammersmith Palais is such a lovely place inside. I used to go and see a lot of reggae bands there in the late Seventies. I saw every name in the reggae world that you could care to mention.**" JOE STRUMMER, 2001

WHITE MAN IN HAMMERSMITH PALAIS

Give 'Em Enough Rope 1978

"Me and Mick met Sandy Pearlman and we went into the toilet and he said, 'What do you reckon?' And we said, 'Let's give it a whirl.' Originally, someone introduced us. I think Bernie Rhodes. One day I was in Bernie's car and he was playing Blue Oyster Cult and I said, 'What are you playing this shit for?' Cos he's usually got some doo-wop or some reggae or something. And he goes, 'Oh, it's well produced' and I said, 'So what? It's a load of shit.' But I'm listening to the production, he said. He was checking it out."

JOE STRUMMER ON HOW THE CLASH CAME TO
WORK WITH PRODUCER SANDY PEARLMAN (1978)

"We had some reservations. We didn't know if we wanted anyone else in the studio with us. A producer's just a translator. They're people with paid ears, wallet ears. They'll listen to what you have and they try to find a way to make sure it sells. But Pearlman's cool. I can learn from him. But if CBS is hoping he's going to compromise our sound, they're going to be surprised."

MICK JONES, 1978

"We arse around so much, you know what I mean. We relax and laugh and joke and if you don't get down to it sometime, you'll never do it." **JOE STRUMMER ON RECORDING THE ALBUM, 1978**

"Mick was at Sandy's shoulder, checking out everything he did."

TOPPER HEADON, 2004

“Sandy's been trying for six months to turn us into Fleetwood Mac. I think he just gave up last night.”
JOE STRUMMER TALKING DURING THE LAST DAYS OF OVERDUBS IN THE U.S, 1978

“By a miracle of God they looked like they believed in what they were doing. They were playing for the thrill of affecting their audience's consciousness, both musically and politically. Rock 'n' roll shouldn't be cute and adorable. It should be violent and anarchic. Based on that, I think they're the greatest rock 'n' roll group around.” SANDY PEARLMAN, 1979

“We're trying to do something new. We're trying to be the greatest group in the world and that also means the biggest. At the same time, we're trying to be radical. I mean, we never want to be really respectable and maybe the two can't co-exist but we'll try. You know what helps us? We're totally suspicious of anyone who comes in contact with us. Totally. We aim to keep punk alive.”
JOE STRUMMER, 1979

“No one's really very scared of punk, especially the record companies. They've sublimated tendencies this art is based on. The Clash see the merit in reaching a wider audience, but they also like the idea of grand suicidal gestures. We need more bands like this as models for tomorrow's parties.” SANDY PEARLMAN, 1979

GIVE 'EM ENOUGH ROPE 1978 ”

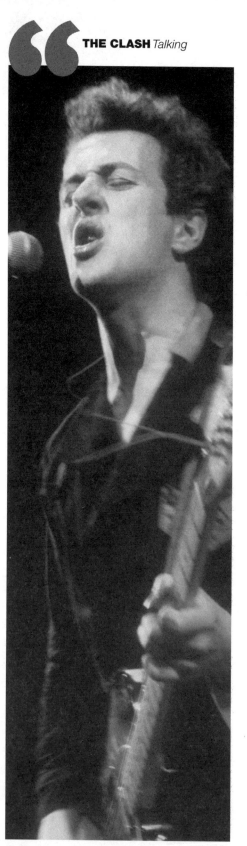

"I could've stood an even worse slagging. The first time you're slagged, it really gets you here, you know. But after that, you get sort of immune. You get a leather heart, you know?"

JOE STRUMMER ON LUKEWARM REVIEWS
FOR GIVE 'EM ENOUGH ROPE, 1979

"It was one of the shouts to refuse to have anything to do with *Top Of The Pops*. It was one of the things we all wanted to do away with, right? It was one of the shouts. No one was gonna do *Top Of The Pops* to sell their records. Seems we're the only ones still shouting. The others have all done it. Maybe they've got their reasons but it makes me sick that it's still on. I want it to end. We won't do it and CB fuckin' S ain't gonna get away with putting any film of us on it behind our backs."

JOE STRUMMER ON ATTEMPTS BY CBS TO
GET A FILM OF THE BAND PERFORMING
'TOMMY GUN', ON *TOP OF THE POPS*, 1979

On Politics

"Marx was something of an old fart. He was an authoritarian and a centralist and what he proposed was essentially the same as capitalism, except with a different set of people in charge. In any kind of realistic political change you have to start on the inside, by changing the central value system. You can't start by changing the structure, change has to be a personal choice." JOE STRUMMER, 1981

"We never thought of what we were doing as political. What all those politicians are up to is what we thought politics was. And when people said we were political, that was what we thought they meant. And we didn't want anything to do with those bastard boring cunts. Who wants to be labelled with that lot of lying bastards?" JOE STRUMMER, 1978

"We're against fascism and racism. I figure that goes without saying. I'd like to add that we're subtle. That's what greatness is, innit? I can't stand all these people preaching, like Tom Robinson. He's just too direct." JOE STRUMMER, 1979

"We're really radical, yeah. We don't do anything we don't want to do. We've got a really high standard that we want to maintain, right? And we don't do anything that might cross that standard. Alright, you've got to sell records to survive because a group is such a huge machine. It requires a lot of money to keep it running. The input of money to keep it going has to come from selling records because you never make money from touring. So we realise we've got to sell records. But we're not prepared to do just anything to sell them. We're only prepared to do what fits in with our idea of what it should be like." JOE STRUMMER, 1979

ON POLITICS

"Our music's violent. We're not. If anything, songs like 'Guns On The Roof' and 'Last Gang In Town' are supposed to take the piss out of violence. It's just that sometimes you have to put yourself in the place of the guy with the machine gun. I couldn't go to his extreme but at the same time, it's no good ignoring what he's doing. We sing about the world that affects us. We're not just another wank rock group like Boston or Aerosmith. What fucking shit."

JOE STRUMMER, 1979

"Don't ask me where my politics came from. I couldn't find anywhere to live. I was willing to wash dishes. I washed plenty of dishes. I dug graves. I cleaned the toilets. I'm not joking on any of these. None of that is an exaggeration. I did exactly what I say. I washed dishes, made omelettes, I dug graves, cleaned toilets. And cut grass in the parks. I did the usual things that young men do. I didn't have nothing behind me. I didn't have nowhere to live."

JOE STRUMMER, 1988

"Toeing any line is obviously a dodgy situation because I'm just not into a policy or I'd have joined the Communist Party years ago. I've done my time selling *The Morning Star* at pit heads in Wales and it's just not happening." JOE STRUMMER, 1981

"When you mention politics now it's like a bad word almost. It's synonymous with corruption and unfairness. At the time it came across as political but we were just talking about what affected our lives. We were never allied in any way to any political party though. Obviously we were from the left and we cared about things and Joe especially taught us all how we should treat people. We learned a great lesson from him. How Joe was, he taught us all." MICK JONES, 2004

66 Hey, you know, we're drug addict musicians. That's what I used to say to journalists: 'Hang on, don't get the wrong idea that we're carrying around *Das Kapital* and loads of pamphlets.' We had Mott the Hoople records and reefer, you know? 99 **JOE STRUMMER, 1988**

66 **Despite Joe's upbringing as a nice middle class boy, they were revolutionaries in their heads.** 99 PHOTOGRAPHER PENNIE SMITH, 2004

66 You're talking about radical acts, right? You mean, like planting bombs. That's a radical act, isn't it? To actually blow something up is an extreme act. There's nothing more extreme you could do to this caff than blow the place up and leave a big hole in Edgware Road. Maybe you could take your clothes off and dance around on the tables. That would be pretty good. That would turn a few heads. But to blow it up would be pretty extreme. But the thing is, we never came to destroy. 99 **JOE STRUMMER, 1979**

ON POLITICS 99

"The only reason I ever brought up people like The Red Brigades was because I couldn't believe what they were doing. They were just, like, normal people, right? And they've taken up guns. They've gone out robbing banks, kidnapping people and shooting people and murdering them and blowing up places. They've gone to that extreme. So I had to compare them to me, right? Right now there's loads of people out in their country mansions getting ready to go grouse shooting. And at the same time there's millions of old age pensioners who have to wrap themselves in bits of cardboard to keep warm because they've got no heating and they have to live for three days on a piece of rotting bread because they've got no food. And I don't think it's fair. And those people in West Germany and Italy, they decided that the only way they can fight it is to go out there and start shooting people they consider to be arseholes. At once I'm impressed with what they're doing and at the same time I'm totally frightened by what they're doing." JOE STRUMMER, 1979

"I've decided from my own personal experience that I do not believe in right wing capitalist pressure groups, governments. I've been fucked up the arse by the capitalist system. I've had the police teaming up with landlords, beating me up, kicking me downstairs, all illegally, while I've been waving Section 22 of the Rent Act 1965 at them. I've watched them smash all my records up, just because there was a black man in the house. And that's your lovely capitalist way of life: I own this and you fuck off out of it."

JOE STRUMMER, 1981

"We felt that the whole machine was teetering on the brink of collapse. Some amazing things went down in Britain during the '70s. The government decided they could disempower the unions by having a three-day week, for instance. Can you imagine that? Everything felt unstable and looking through youthful, excitable eyes, it seemed the very future of England was at stake."

JOE STRUMMER, 2001

Pearl
Harbour '79

"It's time for us to come here (the U.S) with a manifesto of change. All we can do is try. If people can't see what we are - *the* rock 'n' roll band of the '70s – that's their problem." **MICK JONES, 1978**

"If you can't understand the words, don't worry, you're not alone."

JOE STRUMMER TO A U.S AUDIENCE, 1979

"I'd hardly been anywhere before. It was the most exciting thing that ever happened to me. America was amazing for us. We toured with Bo Diddley, travelling on the same bus. He was like our dad. We were protected 'cause he was a deputy or something so we never got in any trouble. If we got pulled over, he'd just get his badge out. You gotta give the man respect."

MICK JONES, 1995

"Rock n roll is played on enemy ground."

JOE STRUMMER, 1979

“ ‘I'm So Bored With The USA’ was the first song we ever
played in America. We were misinterpreted with that song.
We were complaining about the Americanisation of England.
We were always very interested in American culture.**”**

MICK JONES, 2004

BO DIDDLEY

“ It was phenomenal when I met Bo. To ride on a bus with him
and listen to him talk was great. Each man had a bunk on the
bus. I noticed Bo was sitting up late, late, late. So I said, ‘You
know you've got a bunk, don't you, Bo?’ He said, ‘Come and look
at this.’ He pulled back the curtains and his square guitar was
there on the bunk, all strapped up. He went, ‘Guitar rides in the
bunk, I ride in the seat.’ **”** JOE STRUMMER, 2002

“ We insisted on going on tour with Bo Diddley. It was a privilege
for us to bring people like Bo on tour. Most of those people
couldn't get a good gig in America at that time. There's so much
great music in America and it wasn't being treated with the
righteous respect it deserved. **”** **MICK JONES, 2004**

PEARL HARBOUR '79 **”**

On Moving
Away From
Punk

"We're nothing like The Sex Pistols. We don't set out to shock people through being sick onstage or through self-mutilation."

TOPPER HEADON, 1979

"I was never one for sticking a pin in me nose."

MICK JONES, 1979

"We don't walk around with green hair and bondage trousers anymore. We just want to look, sort of, flash these days."

JOE STRUMMER, 1979

The Cost Of Living EP

❝We were in San Francisco doing overdubs for *Give 'Em Enough Rope* and they had the original of this on the jukebox. So when we came home we just started playing it. That's a really good clip of us doing 'I Fought The Law' in *Rude Boy.*❞

PAUL SIMONON ON HOW THE CLASH ENDED UP COVERING "I FOUGHT THE LAW" ON THE COST OF LIVING EP, 2003

COST OF LIVING EP

"**"I was never one for sticking a pin in me nose."** MICK JONES

"Rock n roll is played on enemy ground."

JOE STRUMMER

"We'll probably get together when we're pensioners. You don't get much for the pension these days, do you?"
PAUL SIMONON

"I think about those guys sometimes and hope it didn't f**k up their lives too much." JOE STRUMMER

Rude Boy

"It was a confusing period for us. It's great for the live performances but I remember on many occasions asking the director what the film was about. Mick and Joe certainly asked the same and no-one seemed to have much of a clue. The directors were busking it. As a documentation of the time it's fine, with the rise of the National Front and so on, but it's nothing more than that. The story was a bit weak and the whole situation with the black guys in Brixton, I don't know what they were trying to set up but it was a bit unclear and careless. I didn't even know that stuff was being filmed. The filmmakers generally just followed us around and put the camera on from time to time. There were a few scenes that were staged or based on a loose sketch of a script but that was about it."

PAUL SIMONON, 2004

"It's a fakeumentary. I had no idea how it was gonna end up looking. I was under the impression that the bulk of the stuff was gonna be about The Clash and all these other things with me were just gonna be inserts. But during filming something happened between the filmmakers and The Clash's management and it became much less of a smooth journey."

RAY GANGE, 'STAR' OF RUDE BOY, 2003

RUDE BOY

❝We were making *Rude Boy* just before we started working on *London Calling*. There were a few bits in that film like the 'Rudie Can't Fail' instrumental and maybe an instrumental bit of 'Revolution Rock' as well.❞ MICK JONES, 2004

❝It was okay. We did a lot of dubbing. We spent a lot of time dubbing and ordering out Italian meals. We didn't really act - we were being ourselves, really. The film is more interesting now as a social documentary than it was then. We didn't quite like it then. I think it's 'cos it had too much Mrs. Thatcher in it. But sometimes they show it on Film 4 satellite over here and it doesn't look bad now.❞ **MICK JONES, 2000**

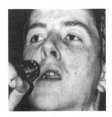

Rehearsals For London Calling

"We'd got rid of our manager Bernie Rhodes which meant we had to leave Rehearsal Rehearsals, which was our base in Camden Town and find a place to start anew. So we decided to send our team on a search for rehearsal studios and they found a place called Vanilla Studios in Pimlico. We block booked it. We had it for the whole summer of 1979." PAUL SIMONON, 2004

"We wrote so much material. A lot of material was never included on the album. We went down to Vanilla Studios in the afternoon and played football, then we rehearsed. *London Calling* was the last album that we actually wrote, rehearsed and recorded.**"**

TOPPER HEADON, 2004

"On some numbers we'd say let's do it reggae style or let's do it rockabilly or in whatever style. I suppose that was probably the beginning of our opening up as musicians." PAUL SIMONON, 2004

"I remember during rehearsals we played football every day, so we were quite fit. Anybody who came along, like any record company guy, they had to play football with us. The teams were normally us against them. It was quite rough 'cos we used to play on concrete.**"** **MICK JONES, 2003**

"All ideas came from the group itself, which was why we were such a tight unit in that respect. This was especially true during *London Calling* because we'd parted with Bernie and left our rehearsal studio in Camden because it belonged to him, the Pistols had split up, Sid Vicious had died and we felt quite alone in some ways. We found the place in Pimlico and became even tighter. In this type of environment you get tighter, to the point where you didn't even need to talk when you were playing because there was a natural communication there."

PAUL SIMONON, 2004

"At the time of *London Calling* we felt most dedicated to our work because we were so close and we'd built up that kind of playing relationship between us."

MICK JONES, 2004

London Calling 1979

"Out of the four of us in the band and [producer] Guy [Stevens] and [engineer] Bill [Price] who worked on the album, Guy and Joe are dead already, y'know? They were both very intense people."

TOPPER HEADON, 2004

"I always loved Guy [Stevens] and he was an incredible catalyst. You'd be in the studio doing a track and he'd come and whisper in your ear. He used to whisper to Joe when he was sitting at the piano, he'd say like, 'Jerry Lee Lewis! Jerry Lee Lewis!' And he'd try to put the spirit of Jerry Lee into the person who was playing. I'd be playing guitar and he used to come up to me and he'd take my headphones off and go like, 'Dion,' in my ear and then put the headphones back on." **MICK JONES, 2004**

"Guy Stevens did go through a period of alcoholism. When we started *London Calling* he was on the wagon and he was taking medication to help him with that but the volition began to fade away as the project progressed. By the end of it, I'm afraid, he'd started drinking again." ENGINEER BILL PRICE ON GUY STEVENS, 2004

"We spent five months rehearsing *London Calling* and went and banged it off in four weeks. The horn parts were all done in one day by the Irish horns, who kind of made up their own arrangements and riffs on the spot. We'd suggest the way it should go, they'd fill it out and bang, it was a part and we banged it down. They hit five tunes from scratch. That's the way we used to do it." **JOE STRUMMER, 1988**

LONDON CALLING 1979

" Joe was playing the piano and Guy came in and poured a bottle of wine into the piano to make it sound better while Joe was playing. " PAUL SIMONON, 2004

" Topper and Mick were the best musicians but Joe had his own guitar style. It was Joe's guitar. He didn't claim to be a great exponent of solos but it was expressive rhythm guitar and he was extremely good at it. One of the ways Joe got that clanging sound was to use a heavy gauge of strings, which was very heavy on the left hand. Joe did have a bit of a problem with wearing his fingers to the bone. " BILL PRICE, 2004

" 'London Calling' was the pivotal track on that album. It's like 'London Calling' is at the top and encompasses all the rest, like an umbrella, like the world in microcosm. With the backwards guitar solo I was thinking of trying to be like The Creation. "
MICK JONES, 2003

" The band were international. They weren't little Englanders. The music was American influenced because it was rock 'n' roll. "
BILL PRICE, 2004

" I did it the night before, I did a demo at home, came in with the song the next morning, into the studio and we recorded it. Just like that. And Chrissie Hynde was upstairs, I was looking up at her through the window, the upstairs lounge, she was there. I recorded the song looking up at her. But it wasn't about her, obviously! There was talk of that. But in the end, we decided to include it on the album but because the artwork had already gone to press, there was no way of putting the title on. That's how it turned out as not being originally on the artwork. "
MICK JONES ON WRITING AND RECORDING 'TRAIN IN VAIN,' 2005

" The song is about an individual's outlook, possibly a paranoid situation. I was living in a basement flat at the time [on Oxford Gardens, W10] and the lack of sunlight can sort of turn your mind. " PAUL SIMONON ON WRITING 'GUNS OF BRIXTON,' 2004

❝Guy Stevens once lay down in front of the head of CBS Records' Rolls Royce. When Maurice Oberstein came to Wessex Studios and listened to a few tracks, he liked it, right, but he didn't say how brilliant it was and so Guy went, 'Right, I'll lay in front of your Rolls Royce and you have to say how brilliant the record is first before I'm getting out of the way of the car.' In the end, Obie, in frustration, said, Ok, it's brilliant and Guy said, 'OK, I'll let you go now.'❞ MICK JONES, 2004

❝Joe had recently been to Spain and it was like some dual bomb campaign. There was a bomb campaign in Spain and a bomb campaign in Ireland at the time, so that led to part of the lyric, I think. But it was as much about Federico Garcia Lorca as it was about the terrorist situation. It was like a musical history lesson.❞

MICK JONES ON THE INSPIRATIONS BEHIND 'SPANISH BOMBS,' 2004

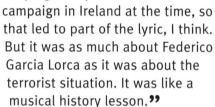

❝Everybody thought I had written that song, but it was actually written by Joe.❞

MICK JONES ON 'LOST IN THE SUPERMARKET', 2004

❝We all like American music. The LP was a hybrid of all our influences. My grounding was in jazz, so we had 'Jimmy Jazz.' My tastes were jazz and soul and a lot of blues and Joe was very into rockabilly at the time, Paul was into reggae and I think a lot of those influences come through on *London Calling*.❞

TOPPER HEADON, 2004

❝It was all about yuppies and how they got into coke.❞

JOE STRUMMER ON 'KOKA KOLA' 1988

> **"We were supposed to be a punk band and yet we were doing whatever we wanted to."**
>
> MICK JONES, 2004

> **"**London Calling was mixed by Bill Price while we were on our first tour of America. We came back and Mick changed one or two tracks a bit but in the main it's Price's mix. I remember a skinhead getting me in Berlin and saying, 'Vot is that? My grandmother like 'Wrong 'Em Boyo'! He was on the edge, he couldn't believe it. He said, 'How could you do something my grandmother likes!' For him the clean sound of that album was a travesty.**"** JOE STRUMMER, 1988

> **"[The cover] was taken at the Palladium in New York. It was towards the end of a two or three month tour. I just twigged Paul looking really pissed off. I thought, that's unusual, he actually looks cross rather than studiously Paul-ish. He just got crosser and crosser. I got my camera ready and thought I'd snap him looking really pissed off if he turned my way a bit and then I saw the bass go up in the air and thought, 'Blimey, that's not the way you play bass.' I took a picture and then one of the crew moved straight in front of me, I think in order to grab the bass. I ducked round him and got the shot just as the bass was on the cusp of coming down."**
>
> PENNIE SMITH, PHOTOGRAPHER OF THE ALBUM COVER
> SHOT OF PAUL SIMONON CLUBBING HIS BASS, 2004

> **"**The night that photo was taken, the frustrating thing was the sound wasn't particularly good and the audience weren't allowed to stand up and dance. When you get annoyed you tend to smash things. Well, I do. Things that you love or whatever.**"**
>
> **PAUL SIMONON ON THE COVER SHOT, 2004**

LONDON CALLING 1979

On The US
Release Of
The Clash 1979

"It was a relief to see it go out 'cos they didn't want it released in the first place." JOE STRUMMER, 2002

"They just held back to see which way it would develop. We came over there and started doing gigs, driving around in a bus. We managed to get known in a huge country through word of mouth.**"**

JOE STRUMMER, 1999

On 'Train In Vain' Becoming An American Hit Single 1980

"*London Calling* was a good record and when it came out in America, people seemed to like it and after that we seemed to take off in America for real. What happened was 'Train In Vain' went on the radio and they thought, 'Wow, this is like totally crossed over' and that really helped us." MICK JONES, 2000

ON 'TRAIN IN VAIN' BECOMING AN AMERICAN HIT SINGLE 1980

Enter Mikey Dread 1980

❝They were real cool. I thought they were poor guys trying to make it. Wrong, they were punks and that was the first time I saw a Punk or heard the word Punk. Being deep into reggae, I was not interested in any other type of music to that level.❞

MIKEY DREAD ON MEETING THE CLASH, 2005

❝Joe Strummer called me up in Jamaica and asked me to come to London and work this song for them. It was a rock song and I turned it into a reggae song. It was a great song, but their record company didn't want to release it so they released it in Germany and it was a huge hit. Eventually, because of the fans, they had to release it in England and it became their first big hit.❞ MIKEY DREAD ON WORKING WITH THE CLASH ON 'BANKROBBER', 2005

❝This blew my mind. I hated the people spitting on Joe and I decided to fight if any of them tried that. They gave me a long black coat and I always stayed way at the back of the stage as I felt it was nasty for any human to show disrespect by gobbing on anyone. If they wanted to see the real Jamaican come out in me then let them try to spit on me. I am glad they never did it or else I would be in jail now doing a life sentence in London for killing one of them for that.❞

MIKEY DREAD ON TOURING WITH THE CLASH, 2005

Sandanista!
1980

"This was a great project which we started by going to Jamaica to do. Then things got out of hand as we selected Channel One Studios on the borders of the ghetto and of course, ghetto people were leaving their homes to see a white band playing reggae and no one could stop them. No one was in danger but I could not see the white faces of the Clash amongst all these black people."

MIKEY DREAD ON THE JAMAICA SESSIONS FOR SANDANISTA!, 2005

"Having The Clash in Kingston was cool, but crazy. Everyone who was anyone kept coming by the studio and finally we couldn't get anything done."

MIKEY DREAD, 2005

"The Jamaican part did not work, so it was moved to the Village at Jimi Hendrix's studio. Then the Rock and Rollers came in to thwart my reggae idea and they won as there were more white people involved. One black man cannot fight off all these punks, so I did a few tracks and that was so."

MIKEY DREAD ON THE
NEW YORK SESSIONS, 2005

SANDANISTA! 1980

❝The recording probably took three weeks or something but I think it took longer than that overall. But it was a three week major bash in there.❞ **MICK JONES, 2000**

❝I was explaining how we were halfway through the mixing and one of the CBS executives said, 'I hope it's not going to be a double album is it, Bill?' I said, '[I can guarantee you it's not going to be a double album.' They said, 'Phew, thank Christ for that.' So I said, 'It's going to be triple.' They said, 'Ha Ha good one!' I don't think they believed it until six sides of *Sandanista!* were delivered to the mastering room.❞ ENGINEER BILL PRICE, 2005

❝That's the gamble we have to take. We believe what we're doing is right. If we had to be dictated by what other people say, it wouldn't be the Clash.❞

PAUL SIMONON ON SANDANISTA! RETAILING FOR LESS
THAN THE PRICE OF A DOUBLE ALBUM, 1981

❝When you release your first record you think, 'Can't wait to hold it in my hand, a piece of vinyl, with a label, a real label.' But you soon dump that. You realise the satisfaction is when you're doing it. It doesn't come later.❞ JOE ON SANDANISTA! GETTING PANNED, 1981

❝The idea was, 'Let's get out there and show all these other groups that they're just ripping all the young people off.' The plan was to give people a whole heap of music and give it to them dirt cheap. We figured we'd show CBS - the mightiest record company in the world - how powerful we were. But we found we weren't all that powerful. CBS showed us that they could put something out on their label and then sit on it just to prove a point. They didn't just not promote it. What's the opposite of promote? They *demoted* it.❞ **JOE STRUMMER, 1984**

❝Punk was about change and rule number one was: there are no rules.❞

PAUL SIMONON DEFENDING THE BAND'S EVER CHANGING MUSICAL SOUND, 1981

❝The problem was that by the time we got to *Sandanista!*, we were touring all the time, we weren't writing and rehearsing. We'd begun to fragment a bit. I'd started doing too many drugs. Mick wanted to record it all in New York so he could be near his girlfriend. We were four very selfish people really. But we still knew that there was this spark there, where we could turn up to the studio with no material and come away with a triple album and all these different types of music.❞ **TOPPER HEADON, 2005**

❝We thought, 'Right, if you want to buy a Clash album that means you want to get into The Clash for whatever reason. So these 36 tracks here are what we've been messing with the past nine months.' So if people want to get into The Clash, this is The Clash and we just laid everything on the table.❞ JOE STRUMMER, 1981

SANDANISTA! 1980 ❞

"Joe was the one with the bigger vision, beyond just the ego of The Clash. Mick was very creative in the studio, like lightning sometimes, but when he took his guitar off he was like a 12 year old. He would like to think he was more important than Joe and Joe would like to think he was important than Mick. But it worked. That was the energy that was The Clash."

KEYBOARDIST MICKEY GALLAGHER, 2005

"I've talked to a few people from El Salvador and I know about the number of people dead or missing. It's running at about 60 a day." JOE STRUMMER, 1981

"It's only films like *Apocalypse Now* that are gonna save El Salvador." **JOE STRUMMER, 1981**

"I suppose really *Sandanista!*, was the end of The Clash as we know them. I guess they lost control afterwards. I don't know what the politics were, but I think it got out of the band's hands. Events were controlling them. They were still coming up with music but there was an element of 'this is where we cash in' about *Combat Rock*. But you've got to move on, haven't you?"

BILL PRICE, 2005

"It's a big flop. The thing I like about making a stand on prices is that it's here and now and not just a promise. It's dealing with reality: how many bucks you're going to have to part with at the counter to get it. It's one of the few opportunities we have to manifest our ideals, to make them exist in a real plane. To do it in Thatcher's Britain during a recession was a kind of flamboyant gesture."

JOE STRUMMER ON THE OUTCOME OF THE SPECIAL PRICING OF SANDANISTA! 1981

On The Reinstatement Of Bernie Rhodes As Manager

"The only pressure is that you're not getting anywhere. You're just standing still. Not making any money. You can't afford to pay the bills. It just wears you down." JOE STRUMMER, 1981

"It was easy to see the problems when I rejoined the group in 1982, but it was another thing to sort them out. They were a lot more serious than I thought. It was like you think to yourself, 'Oh, all we need is a new tire.' Then you discover that they don't make that kind of tire anymore. You have to go to, say, Jupiter, to get it."

BERNIE RHODES, 1982

Tour Of The Far East 1982

❝Topper would invite all these people backstage and they were all drug takers. I remember one time when I was washing my hand and there was all this powder on a mirror. I thought it was just talcum powder. I started to kind of clean up the place and ten hands grabbed me. It was these expensive drugs. It was like carrying a hospital around.**❞** BERNIE RHODES, 1984

❝It wasn't just a puddle. All these huge flies came up out of it! Thousands of huge flies. Next day Paul was like seriously ill and he had to be hospitalised in Bangkok. We were due to go on to the next place but we all agreed we'd all stay. We had a fantastic week, though Paul was in hospital. But the principle was sound. The Clash didn't leave people behind.**❞**

MICK JONES ON SHOOTING THE COVER OF COMBAT ROCK IN BANGKOK WITH PENNIE SMITH, 2005

Combat Rock 1982

“Well, *Combat Rock* were very difficult sessions. There was a bit of friction. When friction builds up people stop communicating or maybe that's the cause of friction. But whatever it is, the result is people don't tell each other what they think anymore. Then you're really in bad water. And we couldn't get out of it. I think that kind of finished us off.” JOE STRUMMER, 2001

“The true genius of 'Rock The Casbah' is Topper Headon. I was in Electric Ladyland studio and he said, 'Look, I've got this tune, can I put it down?' I said, 'OK, Tops, let's put it down.' He ran out in the studio and banged down the drum track to 'Rock The Casbah' and then he ran over to the piano and he banged down the piano track to it and then ran over to the bass and he banged down the bass part. This is, like, I suppose, within 25 minutes and 'Rock The Casbah' is there, boom. Topper Headon did that in 25 minutes.”

JOE STRUMMER, 1988

COMBAT ROCK 1982

" 'Straight To Hell' was all different bits that we had which came together. 'Broadway' was the same, me and him [Topper] doing something at a soundcheck which would suddenly work out." PAUL SIMONON, 2003

" When we kind of got a Top 5 hit with 'Rock The Casbah,' it kind of blew us apart because we figured we must have reached the top of the mountain. And then the struggle wasn't keeping us together anymore. The unity of the struggle. Plus, we'd done too much in too short a time. **"** JOE STRUMMER, 2001

" We didn't think we'd get that far. Was that the beginning of the end? Looking back, yeah, now I realise this is what happens to groups. They grow up together and grow apart. You're under massive pressure. It comes to an end. **"**

MICK JONES ON THE WIDESPREAD SUCCESS OF COMBAT ROCK, 2005

" The lyrics are great. I think part of "Straight To Hell" was what was going on in El Salvador at the time. It was gonna become like Vietnam. The U.S were sending advisors in and all that stuff so we were aware of everything. That Latin feel it's got is probably a subconscious thing cos of what was going on in Central America. **"**

MICK JONES, 2003

" One morning I woke up and we were in [punk band] Discharge! **"**

MICK JONES ON JOE STRUMMER'S
MOHICAN, 1982

COMBAT ROCK 1982

On Joe Vanishing Just Before The UK Tour 1982

❝Joe Strummer's personal conflict is where does the socially concerned rock artist stand in the bubblegum environment of today? I feel he has probably gone away for a serious re-think.❞
BERNIE RHODES' STATEMENT TO THE PRESS, 1982

❝**I just enjoyed buggering about. Being in a rock group as a way of life is not conducive to being responsible. You get treated like a kid.**❞ JOE STRUMMER, 1988

❝It was something I wanted to prove to myself, that I was alive. It's very much like being a robot, being in a group. You keep coming along and keep delivering and keep being an entertainer and keep showing up and keep the whole thing going. Rather than go barmy and go mad, it's better to do what I did, even for a month. I just got up and went to Paris without even thinking about it. I only intended to stay for a few days but the more days I stayed, the harder it was to come back because of the more aggro I was causing that I'd have to face there.❞ **JOE STRUMMER, 1982**

❝**The fact that he went just cleared the air and made you realise more of where you stood individually as well as to two or three other people. I knew he was coming back.**❞ PAUL SIMONON, 1982

On The Sacking Of Topper Headon

"[I'm leaving The Clash] due to a difference of opinion over the political direction the group will be taking.**"**
TOPPER HEADON'S STATEMENT EXPLAINING WHY HE HAD QUIT THE CLASH, 1982

"I think losing Topper had a great effect on us." MICK JONES, 1982

"It was his decision. I think he felt it's not too easy to be in the Clash. It's not as simple as being in a comfortable, 'we're just entertainers' group and he wanted to do that, just play music.**"**
JOE STRUMMER, 1982

"When we knocked out Topper for excessive drug abuse, I don't think, honest to God, we ever played a good gig after that. Except for one night in New Jersey we played a good one but I reckon that was just by the law of averages. Out of a 30 gig tour, one night, you've got to say it's a fluke." JOE STRUMMER, 1988

"We were ignorant. It was like hoo hoo hoo, the big heroin, horse. I didn't know anything about it. It was only after we fired Topper and my friends began to go down like flies. Now most of my friends in London are in Narcotics Anonymous. They can't even have a glass of wine. Just cigarettes and coffee. It's forever. I never liked heroin. I never even took it. I might have smoked it once in Holland. I remember the bloke said, 'Zis next joint has the heroin in it.' I took like a show puff, the one where you keep it in your mouth. And that was the only time I ever got really near heroin.**"**
JOE STRUMMER ON TOPPER'S HABIT, 1988

ON THE SACKING OF TOPPER HEADON

On Terry Chimes
Rejoining

"We had to find a drummer within five days before this tour and we couldn't think of anybody except Terry. We just went for what he knew, so we're playing the old stuff on this tour. I kinda like that old material." JOE STRUMMER, 1982

"I think we're really desperate, really hungry again, because Topper's left and we feel vulnerable again."
JOE STRUMMER ON SUMMER/AUTUMN TOURING WITH TERRY CHIMES, 1982

"Big stadiums are never much fun because you can't see the people you're playing to. But I remember playing 'Career Opportunities' at Shea Stadium in 1982. It was odd, thinking back to when we used to rehearse in a tiny place in Camden and here we are bashing it out in front of tens of thousands."
TERRY CHIMES, 2003

"When Topper went and I rejoined in 1982, "Straight To Hell" was the one song I liked playing live more than the others. Normally I always preferred the faster, harder side of things but because it was slower this was one of the few songs that I could actually sit back and listen to as we were playing. The way Joe sang it he always had so much feeling. The lyrics used to get me every time." **TERRY CHIMES, 2003**

Hell W10

❝Let's make a film! We had no other agenda there than that. Everyone put in their time totally without thinking about it. That was what we did on our time off: we worked! It was totally Joe's idea. He said, 'Let's make a film,' and we made a film. He directed it, he shot it, he did it. And then it was gone. It didn't even come out!❞ MICK JONES, 2005

❝I have directed a film myself. It was called *Hell W10*, a black and white 16 mm silent movie and it was a disaster. Luckily, the laboratory that held the negative went bankrupt and destroyed all the stock, so the world can breathe again. That was like a dry run for me. I managed to shoot it without a script. God knows what it was about. I was the only other one who knew and I'm not telling. But when I get the bug back, I might try another one. I think film directing is something you have to build up to make a few bum films like they do in college. No one has to see it, and then you get your hands on a bit of dough and a good idea, and with a bit of luck you can swing it along from there, learning as you go. Only an idiot would just attempt to walk in and try and direct a picture.❞

JOE STRUMMER, 1987

TERRY CHIMES

HELL W10 ❞

The Beginning Of The End

"The worst moment was realising that there was no way forward, like the gap between the rhetoric and the actuality. For example, talking about all the issues that the Clash raised and what your daily life would have been like if we'd have stayed together. I knew it would tear us apart 'cause I could see after we went Top 5 with 'Rock The Casbah' there was a way for us to sort of smash forward and get up there on a U2-type level, yeah. But then I realised that your whole thing could be get up, interview, video shoot, photo shoot. You know, you'd never really have a life that would be real and yet you'd be expected to say something real about life to real people and make some real sense. You know, sing something really new, and you'd just, you'd end up lying." JOE STRUMMER, 2002

"Those five years from 1977 to 1982 were very intense. Yak yak yak, non-stop yak. I didn't have any more to say because we'd done eight slabs of long playing vinyl inside a five year period. I think I was exhausted: mentally, physically. Every which way.**"**

JOE STRUMMER, 2000

"It was getting harder for all of us at the time. They said I didn't want to tour. It wasn't that I didn't want to tour, I wanted to tour places we hadn't toured before. That came out as I didn't want to tour. I wanted to go other places, go further, and then towards the last days, there was the New Orleans plot. Bernie had been back for a while and he was telling us to play New Orleans music and it was really screwing us up, in rehearsals and everything. And he was saying, 'What record do you want to make, Mick?' And I was saying, 'I want to make a rock 'n' roll record.' But it really affected our relationship right at that point where we were pretty fragile anyway. It threw a massive spanner in the works. And the next thing that happened was I left the group."

MICK JONES, 2005

THE BEGINNING OF THE END

On The Sacking Of
Mick Jones

❝I know that I did behave like a rock star. But in doing that, I was just one component of what made up The Clash. It was never just one person or one attitude: You could see it all onstage, the way we moved around and complemented each other. At first, the effect we had live was all we were after. The three of us at the front knew exactly how it looked to the audience. It was exactly as we wanted. That's why we weren't even bothered how it sounded at first. I did behave like a prima donna, I did pull numbers. But that was the attitude we all learned from Bernie Rhodes, our manager.**❞**

MICK JONES, 1985

❝Mick and Bernie had never got on and Bernie sort of coerced me into thinking that Mick was what was wrong with the scene. That wasn't hard because as Mick will admit now, he was being pretty awkward. Plus my ego was definitely telling me, 'Go on, get rid of him.'❞ JOE STRUMMER, 1986

"I didn't want to fire Mick. I would have done anything not to fire him. But he'd changed. He seemed to think that selling a million records was a big deal. I thought it was okay for progress. Nothing less than we'd worked for, nothing less than we deserved. But not, let's hang up the guitar and relax.**❞ JOE STRUMMER, 1984**

"Mick was my best friend at one time. We were partners and I don't dispense with my partners easily. I have been trying for four years to patch things up. I had gone to the brink 199 times and come back. But things finally had to end. The thing with Mick, and I've said this to his face on numerous occasions, was that he was really with us at the beginning. He really did a lot, a really good tunesmith, really good guitar player. But he became indifferent. He didn't want to go into the studio or go on tour. He just wanted to go on holiday. He just wasn't with us anymore. Finally, he turns up at a rehearsal and I go, 'How have you enjoyed the last seven years?' and he goes, 'All right, why do you ask?' And I say, 'Well, I think it's time for a parting of the ways.'" JOE STRUMMER, 1986

"I arrived in the studio and Topper Headon, who'd already left the group, was there for some reason with Paul and Joe. There was a really different atmosphere from usual, more intense. Joe just said, 'Mick, we've decided we don't want to play with you any more.' I asked Paul what he thought, but he didn't really say anything. So I put my guitar back in the case and stormed out." **MICK JONES, 2005**

"I've been sacked. I don't really know why, but they just sacked me." MICK JONES, 1983

"I don't feel nothing. Don't worry, I'll be all right. Got to keep going." **MICK JONES AFTER BEING SACKED, 1983**

"Joe Strummer and Paul Simonon have decided that Mick Jones should leave the group. It is felt that Jones has drifted apart from the original idea of The Clash."

OFFICIAL CLASH STATEMENT, SEPTEMBER 1983

"Mick Jones would like to state that he feels the official press statement is untrue. He would like it made clear that there was no discussion with Strummer and Simonon prior to his sacking. Jones does not feel that he has drifted apart from the original idea of The Clash and in the future he will be carrying on as in the beginning." **MICK JONES' STATEMENT IN RESPONSE, 1983**

"Sacked is pretty much right. It's awful. It's horrible to get chucked out of your own band. It's the worst thing. Even if I hadn't been chucked out, if the band had come to a natural end, it would have taken me ages to get over it." MICK JONES, 2005

"I did him wrong. I stabbed him in the back. Really, it's through his good grace we got back together and we're going to write together in the future. We cover completely different areas so we're not cramping each other's style. That's a good thing, a rare thing and in the last two years I've learned just how good and rare that is."

JOE STRUMMER, 1986

"The Japanese believe that if you say bad things about other people, then what you say is a judgement on yourself, rather than of the people you are talking about. That's why I don't want to make any character judgements of Joe or Paul. I believe other people will perceive the truth from what they have said about me." MICK JONES, 1985

"Actually me and Joe made up, which didn't take long. We were like family." **MICK JONES, 2005**

"I think that old quote is probably a lot of old tosh actually. I think everyone drifts away. We asked ourselves to do a lot. I counted sixteen sides of long playing vinyl in five years and a thousand gigs and it's too much. We just had to, for the sake of sanity, really."

JOE STRUMMER REFLECTING ON THE STATEMENT THAT MICK JONES HAD GROWN APART FROM THE ORIGINAL IDEA OF THE CLASH, 2001

ON THE SACKING OF MICK JONES

Cut The Crap 1985

"Bernard Rhodes and Kosmo Vinyl, who were the management team, they started directing things behind the scenes. It was at their instigation that we fire Topper Headon just because he'd become a junkie. Which, in hindsight, you think, 'So fucking what? We could have hung with the dude.' But I guess, at the time, no one knew anything about heroin. And then me being burned out, I allowed Bernie and Kosmo to tilt my hand and fire Mick Jones because it wasn't any fun anymore to be around him. So we fired him and Bernard and Kosmo hired these other guys. So, really, I became a play thing in their hands. And I blame myself. I should have realised what was going on. I was burned out though. I was absolutely exhausted. That's my only excuse." **JOE STRUMMER, 2001**

"I went to the mountains in disgust at a certain point and Bernie Rhodes finished the album, christened it and put it out."

JOE STRUMMER, 1988

"They, the 'new' Clash made a record but they sort of gave up the ghost, one by one, during the making of it. Paul bailed out first, then Joe and then Bernie wanted to be where I was in BAD – writing the songs, producing, everything." **MICK JONES, 2005**

"I started thinking, 'This is all my fault, letting this thing happen.' Firstly letting Bernie manipulate me into getting rid of Mick, which Mick helped by being the grumpiest sod you've ever seen in your life, permanently. Then the actual recording process became more and more horrible as I'd realised what I'd done."

JOE STRUMMER, 2000

“It was absolutely atrocious, maybe with the exception of 'This is England.' Joe admitted to me later that the two new guitarists weren't up to it. He and Bernie ended up shouting at them, screaming, 'Can't you do it like Mick did it?'” **MICK JONES, 2005**

“**CBS had paid an advance for it so they had to put it out. I just went, 'Well fuck this,' and fucked off to the mountains of Spain to sit sobbing under a palm tree, while Bernie had to deliver a record.**” JOE STRUMMER, 2000

CUT THE CRAP

Big Audio Dynamite

❝The purpose of this group is to say something positive for all time, something that separates us from those groups that rant on about world destruction, and those that are just palatable and bland. We want to say something positive and not be brow-beaten into toeing the line. On a more personal level, I see what I'm doing as a battle to come up with our new sound. We're sound pioneers. After all, it would be terrible to come up with just another Clash LP.❞ **MICK JONES, 1985**

❝**It didn't feel like being in The Clash. It felt like something different.**❞ MICK JONES, 2005

❝I wanted to do dance music that had guitars. It was part of finding myself after The Clash and not slavishly copying what I'd done before.❞ **MICK JONES, 2005**

❝**A yardstick.**❞
MICK JONES ON DEBUT ALBUM 'THIS IS BIG AUDIO DYNAMITE', 1995

❝The first album was worked out quite a bit in advance.**❞**

DON LETTS ON THIS IS BIG AUDIO DYNAMITE, 1987

❝After working with The Clash for seven years, I'd become unconsciously constricted by all the rules of musicianship that I'd learnt. So what Don does is to open all that up again because he looks at things and sees possibilities in a way that a musician wouldn't. He's incredibly creative and not just in a visual way.❞

MICK JONES ON WORKING WITH DON LETTS, 1985

❝It was basically an accident. He came down to the studio and we just began working.**❞**

MICK JONES ON REUNITING AND WORKING WITH JOE STRUMMER ON NO. 10 UPPING STREET, 1987

❝I figured, hell, if the end result would be better songs, I should swallow my pride, chase Mick down and see if he wanted to work with me again.❞

JOE STRUMMER ON HOW HE ENDED UP WORKING WITH MICK JONES AGAIN, 1987

❝My role with BAD has nothing to do with the accepted notions of producing. What I basically do is create vibes.**❞**

JOE STRUMMER ON HIS ROLE IN THE MAKING OF NO. 10 UPPING STREET, 1987

❝I tried to do something as far away as possible from the Clash. I ended up sort of going too far after that first record. Over a period of time, I sort of forgot what I was good at: guitar chords and melodies. It's like De La Soul, their first album, *3 Feet High and Rising* was brilliant but then they decided that they didn't want to be all flower power anymore and went totally the other way and made *De La Soul Is Dead*. They'd killed off everything that was good about them. In a way, I killed off what I was good at, in order to do something different.❞

MICK JONES ON THE LATER BIG AUDIO DYNAMITE ALBUMS
AND EVENTUAL DEMISE OF BAD, 1995

BIG AUDIO DYNAMITE

On Trying To Get Mick Jones Back

❝I was trying to undo my mistake. But Big Audio Dynamite was taking off, so he just laughed at me.❞ JOE STRUMMER, 2000

❝I was in Nassau. And I'd just done the first BAD album and Joe came looking for me. He came and rode round the island for two days on a bicycle, looking for me. Literally! And he found me and I said, 'Come and listen to the new BAD record.' And we went into the studio and I played him the record and I said, 'What do you think of it?' and he said, very gracefully, 'I never heard such a load of shit in my life and we should get it back together again.' But it didn't seem the right time. We never got back together again but we all became firm friends again very soon after. That was the nicest thing of all about the band. We were great friends again.❞

MICK JONES, 2005

On The Clash Mk II

❝You see the Clash, we feel we've got a mission. We're almost evangelical about it. We really think we're got a mission to bring back real music, dealing with real things, with real meaning. And I know that's what the people out there want.**❞**

JOE STRUMMER, 1984

❝That's why I've got to play every little town, every little dot on the map. I've got to go out there and work. With Mick, I'd give everyone a list of tour dates and I'd be thinking, 'Oh great, we've never been there before!' And I would show it to Mick and he'd throw it across the room. And all your energy suddenly goes.❞

JOE STRUMMER, 1984

❝Obviously in hindsight it doesn't seem like the world gained much cultural information from the episode, from that 18 month period ending about mid-'84. Perhaps it wouldn't have been missed. But we, The Clash Mk. II did have a good time once in the north of England and Scotland on a sort of weird busking tour. It was the weirdest thing, I'll tell ya. Somehow it was more enjoyable walking around with one of these acoustic guitars than having all those trucks following you down the highway loaded with jigs and rigs and hundreds of lights strapped to pylons. We'd just walk into a bar and go, 'Right, we're gonna play,' and the bloke would go okay. We'd say, 'Put the pints up, then.' He'd say 'okay' and we'd pull out the boxes and jam down ten tunes. Then we'd say, 'Where should we go next?' and catch the night bus to Leeds. We'd play anywhere, morning or night. We played under canal bridges, in precincts, bus stops, nightclubs, discos. In Edinburgh we played to 1,300 people without a PA. It was just us five.**"**

JOE STRUMMER ON THE CLASH MK. II'S BUSKING TOUR, 1988

"We should have been out there stomping on The Police or The Rolling Stones and all those heavy metal bands. The Police are just the new Moody Blues and The Rolling Stones, I don't even know what they are any more. But there was all this internal bickering. We couldn't go out and stomp on those other bands when it was all 'bang bang bang' among ourselves."

JOE STRUMMER, 1984

"Poor Joe was under terrible pressure as you could see 'cos he had that funny haircut! You know when he had that Mohican like Travis Bickle? They were touring America and people are going, 'Where's Mick?,' through the dressing room window and he'd go, 'Fuck off! Mick's an asshole!'**" MICK JONES, 2005**

"I was trying to prove that I was The Clash and it wasn't Mick Jones. I learned that that was kind of dumb. I learned that it wasn't anybody except maybe a great chemistry between us four and I really learned it was over the day we sacked Topper and not the day we sacked Mick. There was quite some time between them. We played a whole tour between those times. But it was the day we sacked Tops." JOE STRUMMER, 1988

"Didn't I have a go at flogging a dead horse? I mean, I flogged the horse until I was arrested by the animal society. You wake up and you're over. It's not a bad thing.**" JOE STRUMMER, 1999**

ON THE CLASH MKII

On The Final Clash Split

"When the Clash collapsed, we were tired. There had been a lot of intense activity in five years. Secondly, I felt we'd run out of idea gasoline. And thirdly, I wanted to shut up and let someone else have a go at it." JOE STRUMMER, 1999

"We got called to Paul's house in Ladbroke Grove and Joe told us he wanted to put the old band back together with Mick. The three of us got £1000 then and the promise of more money. It was sad but I think I was relieved. It was doing my head in."

VINCE WHITE, EX-CLASH MK. II, 2005

"I think about those guys sometimes and hope it didn't fuck up their lives too much."

JOE STRUMMER ON BREAKING UP THE CLASH MK. II, 1988

"I took a long breather after The Clash broke up and I had a really hard time about halfway through that. I felt like I'd blown it and that I'd never get up there again and the only thing that got me through was sheer bloody-mindedness. I just won't quit! Every time I think, 'You've had your lot, now just shut up,' a larger part of me says, 'No, there are things you can say better than anyone and you must say them.' Nonetheless, it was a hard time that was compounded by the fact that both my parents died."

JOE STRUMMER, 2001

Joe Strummer On Film

Sid And Nancy 1986

❝ It's more a dialogue between Sid Vicious and a policeman. In the opening of the film there's a policeman looking at Sid and there's no communication. The complete difference between that cop and Sidney interested me. Only the chorus is singing in his voice and he just says he doesn't know what love is. The verses are the cop. The chorus is Sid's answer. It was too scary to go in there. I really wanted to write a song about, Why Was Sidney Vicious? but I couldn't. ❞

JOE STRUMMER ON "LOVE KILLS", THE THEME FROM SID AND NANCY, 1988

Straight To Hell 1987

❝ On *Straight to Hell*, I was pretty nervous but I found just to concentrate would get me by. Simms [Strummer's character] was written for me, like he never changes his clothes. All the time I was working on *Sid And Nancy* and seeing Alex every day, he noticed after a few weeks that I never, ever, changed, because at that time I wasn't certain of anything and decided to stick to the same clothes while I was thinking hard. ❞

JOE STRUMMER, 1987

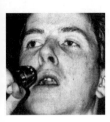

Walker 1987

"Alex Cox and the writer of the film Rudy Wurlitzer wrote parts for me and Dick Rude, another of the veterans from the wonderful *Straight To Hell*, ha ha. We were supposed to be the comic relief from the classy actors. But of course we got cut out, it was classic cutting room floor parts. I felt it would be from the time I got down there. But, after six weeks, Alex turned round to me and said, 'Do the score.' The film took 10 weeks to shoot, I went back to England to sort a few things then went back to Grenada in the south of Nicaragua and wrote the score in weeks and demoed it on my 4-track Fostex." JOE STRUMMER, 1988

"I think this record has soul in it like *Combat Rock*."
JOE STRUMMER ON THE WALKER SOUNDTRACK, 1988

"I liked the work and was particularly proud of one track for a film called *Walker*. I had good musicians and a good understanding with the director. But now I think the enjoyment has gone. The movie companies are ruthless, they want to pay the fee and keep publishing the music. So it's hard, you'll never be able to support your kids doing it. That's why most film music nowadays is generic." JOE STRUMMER, 2000

"I remember having a bit of a chuckle cos the press had written me off after the *Cut The Crap* debacle. The reviews were incredibly reluctantly good. 'This shouldn't be any good but for some reason it seems to be not half bad.' It is a good record. No one's ever heard it but never mind." **JOE STRUMMER, 2000**

Permanent Record 1988

"I think they are all pretty sub-standard. It was a quick knock off job." JOE STRUMMER, 2000

JOE STRUMMER ON FILM

Mystery Train 1989

"I don't sit at home and think, 'OK, what musicians can I get in my next film?' It really happens by accident, in the case of all of those people – Screaming Jay Hawkins, Tom Waits, Joe Strummer, John Lurie. It seems that I tend to hang out with people involved in the music world more than in the film world. And since my work evolves in a kind of organic way, where I start with characters and not with a story, I tend to shape the characters around people I know." **MYSTERY TRAIN DIRECTOR JIM JARMUSCH ON HOW HE CAME TO WRITE A PART FOR JOE STRUMMER IN THE FILM, 1989**

Grosse Point Blank 1997

"Sort of spooky."
JOE STRUMMER, 1997

Mick Jones
On The Near Fatal
Chicken Pox
Attack 1988

❝I had hallucinations. I kept dreaming I was caught up in World War I. I could see the horse drawn artillery and all that.❞ **2005**

❝**It took me a whole six months to convalesce.**❞ 2005

MICK JONES ON THE NEAR FATAL CHICKEN POX ATTACK 1988

The Return
Of Joe:
Earthquake Weather 1989

“There's some great tunes on it like 'Shouting Street,' 'Dizzy's Goatee,' 'Jewellers And Bums,' 'Leopardskin Limousines,' 'Sleepwalk' - those are five tunes that are as good as any tunes on any album by anybody.” **JOE STRUMMER, 2000**

“We did quite a vicious tour, all around America, all around Britain, all around Europe and at the end of the tour I was completely exhausted and the accounts were £24,000 in the red. I remember looking at this sheet and I thought, 'Well why didn't I just sit here and tear up £24,000 and be really fit and happy?'”

JOE STRUMMER, 2000

“Sony (who now owned Strummer's CBS contract) took up the option to make another record. But then they realised that, because I had a descendant of The Clash contract, if I went into a studio that was the contractual signal of them having to cough up the advance. And they realised after *Earthquake Weather* that the advance was way too big for returns. So they were not keen on me to go into the studio at all cos I would kick in a new phase of the contract. I realised, 'Hey, they don't want me to succeed anyway cos it's not in their interests.' So for the next eight years I figured out how to get out of the contract. I realised I was kind of fucked, and I decided to bore them out. I got them to let me go on the grounds that if The Clash ever got back together, then we're contracted to Epic, but on solo stuff I could be free.”

JOE STRUMMER ON THE YEARS OF CREATIVE BARRENNESS THAT FOLLOWED, 2000

Paul Simonon
After The Clash

"I was surprised that it became Number 1. That was quite shocking. And the fact that it was my performance that they had lifted. The smart thing would've been to copy it and change it slightly but they just lifted it straight off. I met up with Norman and we came to an arrangement which was much needed at the time. But I thought it was a really good idea and it was quite reassuring for that to happen to my first song."

PAUL SIMONON ON 'GUNS OF BRIXTON' BEING SAMPLED FOR BEATS INTERNATIONAL'S HIT SINGLE 'DUB BE GOOD TO ME,' 1999

"When I did Havana 3 am, we were veering towards a lot of Latin stuff."

PAUL SIMONON ON HIS SHORT LIVED BAND HAVANA 3 AM, 2004

"There were a lot of people dying and being born around me and I got on the path properly, which meant finding a good teacher and spending years in museums, drawing, drawing, drawing."

PAUL SIMONON ON RETURNING TO ART AFTER HAVANA 3 AM SPLIT UP, 2002

PAUL SIMONON AFTER THE CLASH

That Levis Ad 1991

"It's my first opportunity to use The Clash to lead people into what I'm doing now. I think there's a hell of a lot of Clash fans who don't know what I'm doing. This is the first time we've coupled a piece of music with a reissue. I was asked to put a remix on the other side of 'Should I Stay Or Should I Go Now?' and I didn't want to do that because there's nothing wrong with the originals."

MICK JONES, 1991

"**They (Levi's) didn't give us a single, rotten pair. The world sucks when you get down to the nuts and bolts of it.**" JOE STRUMMER, 2002

Joe In The Wilderness
1990-1999

"I did find it rough, being out of fashion but you have to realise that no amount of slogging around is going to change that. What I should have done is gone to live in France or Spain and got my head together. Coming out of an enormous roller coaster ride like The Clash, you have to get over things.**"** JOE STRUMMER, 2000

"I was intuitive enough to understand: you've had your say, now it's time to shut up for a while. I realised I could cool it. Many performers don't realise the public could do with a rest from some of these seriously ambitious people but the machine grinds on so there's no hope of that happening. I got lucky. I was spat out the back of the machine and fell onto the grass. I had time to say, 'This isn't too bad.'" JOE STRUMMER, 2001

"I had a loss of confidence. I was burnt out after all the excitement of punk rock and what have you. Plus, I'm a lazy son of a gun.**"**
JOE STRUMMER, 2001

"When you take an 11-year breather you have a hill to climb and obviously I've had to deal with a few blows. Forget being on the radio, forget being current, forget MTV." JOE STRUMMER, 2001

Paul Simonon
The Artist

❝I went to the National Gallery, just started drawing. Then it was going outside and painting because I couldn't do it in a studio at that time. It's difficult after you've been on stage, instantly giving people the ammunition they want, to suddenly be on your own. Going outside and painting helped. That, somehow, transplanted the emotions I got from playing in front of an audience. Being exposed to the elements, I felt like I was a human being. When the rain hits your face, you feel you're still alive.❞
PAUL SIMONON ON RETURNING TO ART FULL TIME, 2003

❝**Paul's totally punk rock about his painting. He comes down to my house and paints for hours in the rain. I have to go out with a bottle of brandy to beg him to come in.**❞ JOE STRUMMER, 1999

❝I live in another world now.❞
PAUL SIMONON ON CHOOSING ART OVER MUSIC, 2002

❝**Painting is work. You've got to put the time in. I know what I'm doing and what I need to tackle.**❞ PAUL SIMONON, 2002

❝Sometimes I see a picture in a gallery and I have to run home and paint, the same way that maybe listening to early reggae made you take a bolder step instead of just shuffling along.❞
PAUL SIMONON, 2002

On The Endless Offers To Reform

"People ask why we don't get The Clash back together. One of the things that immediately shoots into my brain is that music has to fit into a certain time and place. Now we have consumed a lot of areas of rock'n'roll that we hadn't in the 1970's and 1980's. You can't keep repeating the same formula. If you plough the same field you reach the bedrock." JOE STRUMMER, 2002

"If my kids were starving, I'd do it. But they're not and I'd like to try and keep my dignity intact so to speak. We'll probably get together when we're pensioners. You don't get much for the pension these days, do you?" **PAUL SIMONON, 1999**

ON THE ENDLESS OFFERS TO REFORM

"Maybe when the heat's off in 20 years time, we'll get together and make a blues record or something. It would be a laugh to do a tour when we're 78. That is a punk rock idea!" JOE STRUMMER, 2001

"We're going to reform when we're 78, we're going to play faster than ever before and we're going to get Wim Wenders to film it. That's what we're going to do. The Buena Vista Clash Club!"

JOE STRUMMER, 2001

"It did get over the top. We were offered millions. Then, like, a million million million. But if The Clash had continued not on our own terms, we would maybe have turned into arseholes. There's a financial cushion because of our heritage, but I have to work, as Joe did, as Mick does. We have our feet on the ground, maybe our heads still in the clouds. It's a good place. Rather than knowing we could retire, buy a swimming pool in the south of France and live off our yesterdays. The nature of The Clash was always to strive forward." PAUL SIMONON, 2003

Joe Strummer
& The Mescaleros

"I had an 11-year layoff. My time to shut up and about halfway through that, I decided I better get up off my ass or it was gonna be too late. So I started to do things: get together with people, record tracks, book sessions. It always ended in disaster, but little by little, I started to meet people to play with. Without people, it's over because you have to get intimate with them. You're not only making music, you're hanging out under stressful conditions. It's even harder than finding someone to marry.**"** JOE STRUMMER, 2001

"We exist in a kind of netherworld beyond MTV where only hipsters venture." JOE STRUMMER ON NEW BAND THE MESCALEROS, 2001

"We've really pitched in together. All hands to the pump. I really appreciate it because there's something human about working as a team. Somehow it brings out the best in humanity and you all pitch in together and you can work without rancour. And you come up with great results. It's pretty gratifying, actually and it ups the quality of the music.**"**

JOE STRUMMER ON CHEMISTRY WITH THE MESCALEROS, 2001

"It's a joy for me 'cause I've been signed to Columbia and Sony. The difference is that these people actually like music. A lot of those big shots, they don't even know. Rent-a-cars, music, insurance: it's amazing the way they swap CEO's. They don't care about people, do they?"

JOE STRUMMER ON BEING CONTENT WITH NEW LABEL, HELLCAT, 2001

"It's run by human beings, which to me is an amazingly new experience.**"** JOE STRUMMER ON HELLCAT, 1999

JOE STRUMMER & THE MESCALEROS

THE ALBUMS

The X Ray Style 1999

"The best career move I ever made was not making any move at all. As years went by, my stock rose, my popularity increased, so I didn't really want to spoil all that by putting out a record but eventually my wife forced me to do this." JOE STRUMMER, 1999

"I have been asked: what kind of music is it? I wanted to say, 'Well, it's the same old shit, but it doesn't sound good, does it?' This is show biz." **JOE STRUMMER, 1999**

Global A Go-Go 2001

❝*Global a Go-Go* is the best record I've ever been involved in, as for personal satisfaction. We've got a new flavour here: funky, organic. I'd hate to be sitting on a record that anybody would understand. I prefer it when we're banging our heads on the wall. It keeps you alive.❞ JOE STRUMMER, 2001

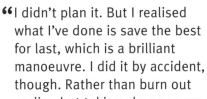

❝I didn't plan it. But I realised what I've done is save the best for last, which is a brilliant manoeuvre. I did it by accident, though. Rather than burn out earlier, but taking eleven years off has turned out to be a not bad idea at all. When the Clash broke up it sort of all fell apart and perhaps that was quite good for my artistic ability, which was a good thing, for me at least.❞ **JOE STRUMMER, 2001**

❝At first I felt isolated and wanted to wait until I'd stopped being the singer from a once famous group, who was this guy who needed help. It was never intentional not to put out a record for so long but in a way it's the best thing that could have happened. It took ten years to recharge my batteries. I didn't want it to be me and a backing band. I wanted to be a member of a group of equals again and I feel collectively we have really hit our stride on this album.❞ JOE STRUMMER, 2002

❝We've made two records in that studio and it took a while for it to sink in, but you go out to get something to eat, buy a newspaper, some honey, a couple of bottles of wine, and you go to about 10 countries. You're into the Sri Lankan deli, the Portuguese café, into the Irish shop, the African grocery store. And all of these people have brought their culture with them. In the Portuguese caff there's

THE ALBUMS

Portuguese MTV, in the African store there's his stuff. In a 10 minute walk you visit 10 countries. And then you're back in the studio. That really began to seep into the records.**" JOE STRUMMER, 2001**

"We've got a kind of grooving, breezy acoustic bass style on some of the tracks. Always grooving. A very heavy drum and percussive section, where we're trying to investigate all of the rhythms of the world without getting stuck on one identifiable form from the past. And on others we go wild with an electronica vibe. However always with a groove, no house beats or anything like that, because we're trying to forge our own style. We try to throw it all in. Every flavour was thrown into the pot and somehow it gelled. It's not a soup that tastes bad. It's a soup that you go, 'Mmm, another bowl of that'." JOE STRUMMER, 2001

"The past is past. I always feel to live in the present. Blank piece of paper is always the same. You've got to fill the blank piece of paper. It's crazy. You've got to face up to your past. It can feel like a millstone in that situation but mainly, I feel proud about it. It's a good spur to try and top that. I don't really dwell upon it. You can't throw yourself off too much. It's great to live in the moment and not think too much about the past. It can really drag you down. I would say the past is like treacle. It can get stuck on your feet if you go back. Can't get in and out that easy. Dylan said, 'Don't look back.'**" JOE STRUMMER, 2001**

Streetcore 2003

"It is infuriating to realise that the most maddening of cliches has come to be true, which is that *Streetcore*, Joe's last record, is probably his best." BONO, 2003

On The
Mick Jones /
Joe Strummer
Live Reunion 2002

"I did get to play with Joe one last time a few weeks before his death. I went along to a striking fireman's benefit in Acton, London, to see the show and I had no intention of getting up but when I heard Joe and the Mescaleros start 'Bankrobber' I felt compelled. And of course it was a fireman's benefit so we played 'London's Burning' at the end. It was very much like our old days: a town hall and it was for something we felt was important. It somehow seemed right.**"** MICK JONES, 2004

"When we were still in The Clash, there were times I didn't want to play 'White Riot.' We used to argue about it. Joe still wanted it in the set and I thought its message had been lost over the years. So we were on stage for the first time in ages at this firemen's gig and Joe looked over at me and shouted, 'You know it,' and made an A-chord sign, which was our signal for 'White Riot.' I had no choice but to join in. It was lovely to be back on stage and enjoying it." MICK JONES, 2004

ON THE MICK JONES / JOE STRUMMER LIVE REUNION 2002

The Death Of Joe Strummer

"Joe phoned the night before he died. He was trying to send a fax. It wouldn't go through. So he phoned to say, 'Happy Christmas, I'm trying to send this fax.' I got the fax later. The discussion was, 'Well, are we gonna play the Hall of Fame or are we not?'**"**

PAUL SIMONON, 2003

"It's taken Joe's death to make me realise just how big The Clash were. We were a political band and Joe was the one who wrote the lyrics. Joe was one of the truest guys you could ever meet. If he said I am behind you, then you knew he meant it 100 per cent." TOPPER HEADON, 2003

"Our friend and compadre is gone. God bless you, Joe.**"**

MICK JONES, 2002

Induction To
The Rock 'n' Roll
Hall Of Fame 2003

"The Clash's contribution to the story of rock and roll is immense. Their contribution to the survival of rock and roll I think is unique. When punk was starting to wane mainstream rock had become hopelessly and awfully redundant. The Stones had gone to disco, by the way, where most of the smart money was going at the time. The Clash, along with one or two other bands alone carried the torch. They broke through barriers of perception and genre and left behind them a thousand bands from garage land who caught a glimpse of what they saw and strove for, including one from Ireland called U2." THE EDGE, INDUCTION SPEECH

"By a chance meeting with Mick Jones and Bernie Rhodes, I was suddenly in the group that became The Clash. From 1976, the next eight years were exciting and explosive, both on and off stage. Mick, Joe and me were like The Three Musketeers, brothers in arms fighting to get our message across. After achieving international recognition, we disbanded and went our separate ways."

PAUL SIMONON'S ACCEPTANCE SPEECH ON BEHALF OF THE CLASH.

"They combined revolutionary sounds with revolutionary ideas. Their music launched thousands of bands and moved millions of fans and I cannot imagine what my life would have been like without them. During their heyday they were known as the only band that matters, and 25 years later, that seems just about right to me." TOM MORELLO OF AUDIOSLAVE/ RAGE AGAINST THE MACHINE, INDUCTION SPEECH

Carbon / Silicon

MICK JONES WITH CARL BARÂT FROM THE LIBERTINES

❝Even before Tony (James) and I formed this group, we wondered, 'What are we gonna do? We're going to be 50 year old guys. We don't want to pretend to be kids. We want to be ourselves.'❞

MICK JONES, 2005

CARBON / SILICON

The Legacy Of The Clash

"We achieved more than we ever hoped for or expected."

MICK JONES, 2005

"I see Joe Strummer as a leader in the rock world who never got the recognition that he deserved for his upfrontness, addressing issues that other people were reluctant to address.**"**

MIKEY DREAD, 2003

"I think the reason we were successful at combining rock with reggae or whatever was because each member of the group had a certain background and everybody brought in a different ingredient. I suppose it's like making a cake." PAUL SIMONON, 2004

"Joe spoke the truth and that's important. People seem to respond to that.**" MICK JONES, 2005**

"I wouldn't put us in any punk Top 10, really, because we were wider than that. We ended up playing 'Rock The Casbah,' kind of funking it up. If we were a spaceship, we'd have tracked right out into the galaxy in a straight line. You couldn't get from 'Janie Jones' to *Sandinista!* quicker if you tried." JOE STRUMMER, 1999

"When I heard Rancid, I didn't hear Clash, I heard our common legacy. Because this has got to be traced back to The Ramones. The Ramones' first album really is the blueprint for punk rock. In my estimation, everything about it almost defines punk. So any other group from the release of that album onward is really copping to The Ramones.**" JOE STRUMMER, 1999**

❝We never got any money. The music business is a bad racket and the people on the first crest of a wave never get paid. I don't like to moan on about money but you have to realise that although you might've heard of The Clash, we didn't sell any records. Nobody sends me five pounds every time somebody's heard of the group.❞ JOE STRUMMER, 2001

❝Clash royalites are enough to live on but there are good and bad years. Normally, people gauge their outgoings by their incomings. Unfortunately, from one year to the next, you never know what your incomings are. It's a strange way to live.❞ **JOE STRUMMER, 2002**

❝Every time we did a record it was completely different from the one before.❞ MICK JONES, 2005

❝The modern '80's definition of 'made it' is filling the 100,000 seat stadiums. U2 do five a week. Back then there was still some vestige of a true underground feeling. The Clash had a surge in that area. You saw us in arenas, but we were at our finest with 3,000 people in an old theatre. If I was to find a mean average of all the 10,000 Clash shows there ever was, I'd say that 3,000 rocking people in a dirty old theatre in the bad part of town is the mean average. And that ain't even making it. You know what I'm saying? Who's made it? Madonna, Michael Jackson, Prince, U2. We're talking super stadiums. At the high level of the Clash's popularity we could fill the 10,000 seat hockey arenas or gyms. You only ever saw us in a big place if it was a festival or we where supporting the Who. And if you look at our record sales, nothing sold until _Combat Rock_ and 'Rock The Casbah.' I'd say we sold a speck overall to what U2 sell now.❞ **JOE STRUMMER, 1988**

❝Joe taught us all a lot. And the main thing he taught us, not that we didn't know it, was how to be with people. He was a man of the people. And I couldn't just give you one example of that. He was like that all the time.❞ MICK JONES, 2005

❝The Clash was always from the heart. No matter if it went down or up, it was always from the heart.❞ **JOE STRUMMER, 1988**

THE LEGACY OF THE CLASH